CW00954236

EARLY POEMS AND JUVENILIA

Philip Larkin

Early Poems and Juvenilia

EDITED BY

A. T. TOLLEY

faber and faber

First published in 2005
by Faber and Faber Limited
3 Queen Square London WC1N 3AU
Published in the United States by Faber and Faber Inc.
an affiliate of Farrar, Straus and Giroux LLC, New York

Photoset by RefineCatch Ltd, Bungay, Suffolk
Printed in England by T. J. International, Padstow, Cornwall

A CIP record for this book
is available from the British Library

ISBN 0–571–22306–0

2 4 6 8 10 9 7 5 3 1

Contents

[vii]

[x]

Acknowledgements

My first debt to be acknowledged is to Philip Larkin himself, who encouraged me in the early eighties in my first explorations of the records of his early poems, and who kindly read what I then wrote about them. I owe a great deal to Larkin's Literary Executors, Anthony Thwaite and Andrew Motion, who kindly gave permission for the preparation of this collection. I have particularly benefited from Anthony Thwaite's 1988 edition of the *Collected Poems*, which has been a model for this collection; and from Andrew Motion's *Philip Larkin: A Writer's Life*, which has been a valuable source of information and background. The identification and bringing together of the poems in this book would not have been possible without the lists of material in the Larkin archive at the University of Hull prepared by the Archivist, Dr Brian Dyson. His advice has also been of special value. Valuable advice was also given by Dr James Booth of the Larkin Society.

Some of these poems have previously appeared in Anthony Thwaite's 1988 edition of the *Collected Poems*. A few others have appeared in *About Larkin*, published by the Larkin Society.

My wife, Dr Glenda Patrick, assisted in the arduous task of checking the texts. Initial reproduction of the texts was done by Tunnel Graphics of Carleton University. Text preparation was carried out by Christina Thiele of Carleton Production Centre. I am grateful to Matthew Hollis and Charles Boyle of Faber and Faber for further editorial work.

I am specially indebted to the Social Sciences and Humanities Research Council of Canada, who made me a research grant in support of this work.

A. T.

Introduction

The high acclaim and extensive sales of Larkin's *Collected Poems* showed that he had become one of the most admired and loved English poets of the twentieth century. His poems have indeed established themselves as among the major poetry of the period in English. His writings have been the subject of many studies and many learned gatherings; and his poems are part of the curricula of schools and universities. For these reasons alone, everything he wrote should be available to those who study his work; while everything he wrote is of interest to his admirers.

Almost all the poems that Larkin completed after 1950 were published by him; and they were included in the original *Collected Poems*. However, while Larkin completed about a hundred and sixty poems between 1950 and his death in 1985, he wrote over two hundred and fifty poems between 1938 and 1946. The earliest of these belong to Larkin's years at King Henry VIII School in Coventry; and the first included here would seem to have been written before he wrote School Certificate – the examination that later became 'O' levels – in 1938, when he was sixteen.

Among the papers left by Larkin was an early account of his writing. His earliest writings were short stories or sketches; but, in the summer of 1938 he 'began to write poetry of a descriptive kind, about trees and the sky and the seasons'.[1] He gave as a sample, 'Winter Nocturne', the first of his poems to be published – in the school magazine, *The Coventrian*, for December 1938. He said then of this early poetry, 'It is not in imitation of anyone: in fact, I did not read poetry at all. Through the winter of 1938–9 I continued to write poems, all much of the same kind, faintly influenced by Keats and Aldous Huxley, until in the spring I broke into freer verse when I re-fell in love with someone. Then poems became more personal and more frequent . . .'[2] During the summer of 1939 he evidently began his practice of making small collections of his poems in typed, stitched pamphlets, the first being The Happiest Days. 'Before 1939 was out', he goes on to say, 'the war had started and I wrote two more books of poems. One was "Poems in War" (Sept. 3rd–Oct. 7th). These poems were influenced by the modern Left-wing school, generally whom I read avidly, especially Auden. It included a masque: "Behind the Facade", which I'll keep. "One O'Clock Jump" the other was called, not that the titles had anything to do with the contents. Towards the end they became gritty.'[3] The comment about the titles reflected the fact that 'One O'Clock Jump' was the title of the most famous recording by the Count Basie Orchestra, which Larkin so much admired. Influences such as that of T. S. Eliot creep in in poems such as 'When the night puts twenty veils'; and Eliot is an acknowledged model in the notes appended to poems in Larkin's first surviving and untitled typewritten collection.

From the summer of 1939 to August 1942, Larkin in fact produced ten typewritten collections of his work: The Happiest Days (Summer 1939); Poems in War (October 1939); One O'Clock Jump (October 1939); [Untitled Collection] (Late 1939); The Village of the Heart (28 March 1940); Further Poems (July 1940); Poems, August 1940 (August 1940); Chosen Poems (April 1941); Seven Poems (January 1942); and The Seventh Collection (July 1942). The pace seems at times rather hectic: about two hundred poems in three years; while the volume from August 1940, containing nineteen poems, was brought together only a month after the previous one. His departure to Oxford in October 1940 seems to have slowed things down. He made a retrospective 'chosen poems' in the following April; and the final two collections are rather brief, perhaps indicating that the literary competition at Oxford, and the experience of actually appearing in print there, may have caused Larkin to take a more objective view of his earlier fluency.

The first three collections no longer exist – probably destroyed by Larkin, who not long after they were made went over much of this earlier work, writing in abusive comments. However, in the early narrative of his writing Larkin includes over thirty of these poems that he then liked, as well as some fragments. He in fact used one of the poems, 'The Days of thy Youth', in the first extant collection; and seven more in the second extant collection, The Village of the Heart.

Auden was an important shaping influence, which seems to show itself as early as with the sonnet 'Having grown up in shade of Church and State', written on 9 June 1939. During 1940 there are many poems by Larkin directly based on poems in Auden's volume of 1936, Look Stranger!, a book that Larkin continued to admire throughout his life. The title of Larkin's collection The Village of the Heart is taken from a poem in that book. 'Out in the lane I pause: the night' clearly echoes the opening line of the second poem in Look Stranger!, 'Out on the lawn I lie in bed'; while its stanza form seems to derive from another poem in that book, 'Brothers, who when sirens roar'. In its attempt at a panoramic view of England, 'Midsummer Night, 1940' recalls the 'Prologue' to Look Stranger!; while the many potted narratives in sonnet form take their example from Auden's repeated use of the sonnet in this way in the nineteen-thirties, as in poems such as 'A shilling life will give you all the facts'. When Larkin came to leave school, he and Noel Hughes wrote 'Last Will and Testament' – a poem of farewell based on a poem with the same title written jointly by Auden and Louis MacNeice, in their book Letters from Iceland, published in 1937. In many respects, this Audenesque vein was Larkin's best in these early years; and the lessons of Auden were to remain with him throughout his career.

By the time Larkin was in his first term at Oxford, one of his poems, 'Ultimatum', had been published in The Listener for 28 November 1940. Some of his poems appeared in undergraduate periodicals; but the admiration of Auden, obvious in almost all he wrote at the time, was not to his advantage. Poetry circles at Oxford at the time were dominated by Sidney Keyes, who, with Michael Meyer, edited a principal undergraduate literary magazine, The Cherwell. In 1941 Keyes and Meyer brought together a collection, Eight Oxford Poets, for Herbert Read at Routledge, in which Keyes describes the contributors as '*Romantic* writers . . . we have, on the whole, little sympathy with the Audenian school of poets'[4] – this despite the inclusion of poems by his friend Drummond Allison, whose admiration for Auden is clear in his work. Keyes did not include any poem by Larkin.

A little before Larkin left Oxford in the summer of 1943, opportunities for publication in book form appeared. Before the war, *Oxford Poetry*, an annual anthology produced by Blackwell, had been one avenue of publication for undergraduate Oxford poets. It had ceased publication at the beginning of the war; but in 1943, its single wartime issue, *Oxford Poetry 1942–43* appeared, edited by Ian Davie. Three poems by Larkin were included: 'I dreamed of an out-thrust arm of land'; 'Mythological Introduction – A white girl lay on the grass'; and 'A Stone Church Damaged by a Bomb – Planted deeper than roots'.

At about the same time, Charles Hamblett attempted to get together a collection of Oxford poetry for publication by the Fortune Press. Nothing came of this; but later William Bell arranged with R. A. Caton, owner of the Fortune Press, to bring out a collection, *Poetry from Oxford in Wartime*. It appeared in 1945. Nine poems by Larkin were included: 'All catches alight'; 'The moon is full tonight'; 'The horns of the morning'; 'I put my mouth'; 'The bottle is drunk out by one'; 'I see a girl dragged by the wrists'; 'Love, we must part now: do not let it be'; 'Morning has spread again'; 'Heaviest of flowers, the head'. The preparation of the collection was followed by a suggestion from Caton to contributors that they might like to submit a volume of their own for publication.

Caton's Fortune Press was somewhat unusual. He had begun in the fine printing field, but had moved into the publication of mild homosexual pornography. In the nineteen-forties he appears to have spotted the opportunity to make some money out of the publication of poetry. He seems to have paid no royalties, though he asked for no money. However, some poets – but probably not Larkin and his friends – were required to guarantee to take a certain number of copies. Caton seems only to have bound up sheets as sales called for books to be available – in some cases, hardly at all. At any rate, he put out Larkin's first published volume of poetry, *The North Ship*, in July 1945; and in 1946 he published Larkin's first novel, *Jill*.

In the meantime, a decisive change had taken place in Larkin's poetry with the visit in 1943 of Vernon Watkins to the English Club at Oxford. Watkins talked about Yeats. 'His reading was a revelation: unashamedly sonorous . . .'[5] Larkin recalled. '. . . I spent the next three years trying to write like Yeats . . .'[6] *The North Ship* showed strongly the results of that change. It consisted mainly of poems that Larkin had written between October 1943 and October 1944. Some of them, such as 'To write one song, I said', contain blatant imitations of Yeats. What redeems many of them is the delicate and unerring control of movement, which was a gift manifest in almost all of Larkin's poetry. The book, like most of the volumes that the Fortune Press put out, received little attention.

At the end of 1943, Larkin was looking for a job. He was medically unfit for military service, but required by the Ministry of Labour to do work of an approved kind. He had been rejected by the Civil Service. He obtained a job as a librarian in Wellington in Shropshire, where he began work on December 1st. Shortly after he went to Shropshire, he began composing in the first of his 'workbooks', though the first remaining entry is the poem 'If grief could burn out' in October 1944. From then on he seems to have composed all his poems in these workbooks, bequeathing to us an unusual record of the composition of the work of a major poet. He later somewhat facetiously described his literary activities in Wellington: 'Every night after supper before opening my large green manuscript book I used to limber up by turning the pages of the 1933 plum-coloured Macmillan edition [of Yeats] . . .'[7] The poems rather bear this out, as the influence of Yeats is very obvious in the sixty or so poems composed in the three years after he arrived in Wellington.

In 1947, Larkin brought together another collection of poems, In the Grip of Light. The vague, idealistic tone of the title, with its near oxymoron, gives a sense of what to expect from this volume that showed, again, the marked and poorly absorbed influence of Yeats. The book was seen by many publishers, including Faber's T. S. Eliot. Despite the fact that Faber had taken Larkin's second novel, *A Girl in Winter*, nobody wanted to publish Larkin's poems.

In the Grip of Light marked the end of Larkin's poetic misdirections. He has described the changes that came over him in those days: 'One book I had at my bedside was the little blue *Chosen Poems of Thomas Hardy*';[8] and, as he read Hardy, 'it was with a sense of relief that I didn't have to try to jack myself up to a concept of poetry that lay outside my life . . .'[9] He wrote very little in those years of change between 1946 and 1949. In 1965, in his introduction to the second edition of *The North Ship*, he pointed to the poem 'Sunday Morning', from December 1947, as marking the end of his fascination with Yeats – 'the Celtic fever abated and the patient sleeping soundly'.[10] Emotionally and stylistically, however, one might view the two poems he wrote at the time of his father's death, in March 1948, as showing a more marked change of orientation in the direction of a poetry that took its cue from the emotions evoked by experience, rather than from a romantic desire to create literature – a commitment to experience that was to remain a touchstone of Larkin's poetic activity for the rest of his career. Those poems were 'April Snow', from April 1948, and the following perhaps uncompleted lines, touching in their directness and loving inclusion of detail:

> And yet – but after death there's no 'and yet'.
> Now we have seen you die; and had you burned,
> I cannot aphorise 'what I have learned'
> As neatly as I sort your desk, and set
> The calendar for days you will not see.
> 'Death doesn't do you harm,' you chanced to say
> One morning on the lawn, and straightway
> Fear, young and furtive, took its roots in me

Which in these empty days now comes of age.
And yet – because in life there is 'and yet' –
What can I hope, except that you were right?[11]

In 1949, with the drafting of 'Deceptions' and 'At Grass', a very different attitude to poetry and the craft of poetry finally emerged. 'At Grass', a poem of thirty lines, took twelve pages to draft in the workbook. Larkin's mature style and his mature manner of writing had arrived. Almost every poem he completed after that time was collected by him and appears in the original *Collected Poems*.

The present volume contains all the poems that Larkin completed up to and including the compilation of his unpublished book, In the Grip of Light.

A. T. Tolley

NOTES

1. Hull University Archive, DPL (2)/1/1/10.
2. DPL (2)/1/1/10.
3. DPL (2)/1/1/10.
4. Foreword, *Eight Oxford Poets* (London: Routledge, 1941), vii.
5. Larkin, P., 'Vernon Watkins: an Encounter and a Re-encounter' in *Vernon Watkins 1906–1976*, ed. L. Norris (London: Faber and Faber, 1970), 28.
6. Larkin, P., Introduction, *The North Ship*, 2nd edition (London: Faber and Faber, 1966), 9.
7. Larkin, P., Introduction, *The North Ship*, 10.
8. Larkin, P., Introduction, *The North Ship*, 10.
9. Larkin, P., 'The Poetry of Hardy', *Required Writing* (London: Faber, 1983), 175–6.
10. Larkin, P., Introduction, *The North Ship*, 10.
11. Hull University Archive, DPL (2)/1/1/14.

Abbreviations

The collections that Larkin made, published or unpublished, up to and including In the Grip of Light (1947) are listed in Appendix 1, along with their contents. The following abbreviations are used in the body of the book:

[Untitled first collection]	1st COL
The Village of the Heart	VOH
Further Poems	FP
Poems, August 1940	PAug40
chosen poems	CHP
SEVEN POEMS	7P
the seventh collection	7COL
Sugar and Spice	SS
Poetry from Oxford in Wartime (1945)	POW
The North Ship (1945)	TNS
In the Grip of Light	ITGOL
XX *Poems* (1951)	XX
The Less Deceived (1955)	TLD
Collected Poems (1988)	CP
Selected Letters (1992)	SL
Trouble at Willow Gables (2002)	TWG
About Larkin	AL
Manuscript	MS
Typescript	TS
First Workbook	WKBK

Note on the Sources and Dating

SOURCES

There are three main sources for Larkin's early poems: the poems he published himself; the poems he left in typescript; and the poems in his first manuscript Workbook. Those which he published appeared in the magazine of his school, *The Coventrian*, in various undergraduate periodicals and anthologies at Oxford, and in his first book of poems, *The North Ship*, published by the Fortune Press. Few of these were published more than once. There is no question that these printed versions constitute Larkin's final versions. In the case of the poems that have survived in typescripts kept by Larkin, there are very few of which we have more than one copy; determination of which are the latest versions among these few is not difficult. The typescripts include Larkin's compilation of the unpublished volume of 1947, In the Grip of Light, which again has authority. Finally, the completed poems that survived solely in manuscript in the first Workbook give us final versions in Larkin's hand; and the text that constitutes a final corrected version is always indicated by Larkin's having dated that version. The poem can then be constructed from his corrected manuscript text. There are only a few poems included here from manuscript versions other than those in the Workbook. The printed versions clearly have precedence over other versions; while, given Larkin's usual procedure of transferring a poem to typescript when he was satisfied with it, typescripts have precedence over manuscript versions.

Manuscripts and typescripts of unpublished poems, including the booklets prepared by Larkin, are to be found in the Larkin Archive, Brynmor Jones Library, University of Hull. The First Workbook is in the British Library.

The dating of the poems can first of all be ascertained from the Workbook, if the poems appear there, as Larkin fairly meticulously gave the day, month and year of completion below completed versions. Most of the typescripts come from small collections of poems that Larkin made as a youth or young man; and these collections are mainly dated, though the poems in them are only in a few cases dated. Larkin's narrative of his early writing that survives in manuscript is also helpful in dating early poems, particularly from the collections no longer extant. Further information is found in the associated 'Intellectual Diary'. Some of the other poems in typescript are dated, or appear in typescripts that include poems that can be dated from other sources. The poems that appear in periodicals and books give a terminal date for their composition; and it can be generally supposed that the poems were composed fairly shortly before their appearance. The same may be said of poems included in letters, notably to Larkin's friend James Ballard Sutton. Some in *The North Ship* appear in the first Workbook, as do all those in In the Grip of Light, and their date is given in the Workbook. The poems as printed here are always the latest versions known. Below the printed poems a note is given of all existing versions.

The following convention has been adopted concerning dating. Dates of poems given in any way by Larkin are *not* given in square brackets; while dates deduced *are* in square brackets. If the deduced date is based on the date of publication or date of inclusion in a collection, this basis is not noted. If there is any other basis for dating, this is noted.

SEQUENCE OF POEMS

Many of the dates given are dates before which the poems in question must have been written. These dates are usually based upon the dates of compilation of the collections in which they appeared. The sequences of the poems in the early collections seem often to be chronological – explicitly in the case of 'chosen poems' – and these sequences have been followed where there is nothing to contradict them. To some of the poems in these early collections a definite date of composition may be ascribed from other sources; but these poems have been left in the sequence in which Larkin placed them where this is consistent with the exact dating. For some poems surviving in loose, undated typescript, the dating is vague and based on little or no evidence except the style of the poems; and in these cases the placing of the poems in sequence is conjectural.

POEMS

Spring 1938–December 1946

Coventria

We are the school at the top of the hill,
   That Henry the King did will,
If he came back and saw it now
   The sight would make him ill!
The Heads [*sic*] a lout – Hardy's a weed
   With his lop-eared, pop-eyed gaze
'Up the scrubbers and kick 'is teeth!'
   Will haunt us to the end of our days!

On field or in room, wherever we may be,
   When the print our eyes do maim,
We are bawled at, screeched at, yelled at, too,
   By the scum of the teaching game –
Saints aggressive jaw – Phips squeaky voice
   As he elucidates Vergils [sic] lays . . .
'Nah then, Fahve E 1, yew shoot up!'
   Will haunt us to the end of our days!

When we look back, in the years yet to be,
   And our days live again in thought,
There's one old figure that atones for all the rest
   Tho' throughout the school you sought –
The Grand Old Man, with Bunyan on high,
   It like a banner he does raise . . .
'Oh, well, gud luck to ye all – GUDBYE!!!!'
   Will haunt us to the end of our days!

[*early 1938*] TS (in a letter to Colin Gunner; this letter refers to
Larkin's studying physics, a subject he studied only up to the
School Certificate examination, taken at the age of 16.)

[3]

Winter Nocturne

Mantled in grey, the dusk steals slowly in,
Crossing the dead, dull fields with footsteps cold.
The rain drips drearily; night's fingers spin
A web of drifting mist o'er wood and wold,
As quiet as death. The sky is silent too,
Hard as granite and as fixed as fate.
The pale pond stands; ringed round with rushes few
And draped with leaning trees, it seems to wait
But for the coming of the winter night
Of deep December; blowing o'er the graves
Of faded summers, swift the wind in flight
Ripples its silent face with lapping waves.
The rain falls still: bowing, the woods bemoan;
Dark night creeps in, and leaves the world alone.

The Coventrian, December 1938 CP

Fragment from May

Stands the Spring! – heralded by its bright-clothed
　　Trumpeters, of bough and bush and branch;
Pale Winter draws away his white hands, loathed,
　　And creeps, a leper, to the cave of time.
Spring the flowers! – a host of nodding gold,
　　Leaping and laughing in the boist'rous wind,
Tinged with a yellow as yet not grown old,
　　Green and yellow set against the soil.
Flowers the blossom! – loaded, swaying arms
　　Of sated stalks, heaped with pink and white
Of fresh youth's cheek; they lightly throw their charms
　　Into the fragrance of the deep, wet grass.

The Coventrian, December 1938 CP

[5]

Thought Somewhere in France 1917

The biggest joke in History, I think,
Was the China War, of 1840 Anno Domini,
For the reason of our agression
Was a high moral disgust with dope.
Is spiritual dope better than physical dope?
If so, the newspapers are safe;
And so is this sergeant who is bringing along
The rum ration; for we must go over the top.
You must dope men before they will murder for you.

[*?Winter 1938/39*] TS

'The sun was battling to close our eyes'

The sun was battling to close our eyes
with his thick hot fingers

Faraway there was the flicker of a hand
a laughing glance

       All life flowered
Under the dusty trees.

[*Winter? 1938–9*] CHP (quoted in a letter to J. B. Sutton,
16 April 1941)

Butterflies

Side-stepping, fluttering, quick-flecking,
   dropping like tops under the blue sky
Skipping white under the sultry pall of green
   summer trees
Or side-slipping over rich green hedges
   of cottage gardens, with red and
   yellow flowers
Of the sun, white robed in linen,
Priests of the golden sun, dancing because
   the sun says to them: Dance, that ye
   need no other day
Butterflies, tossing their hours away
   like honey drops.

Darling, when in the evening I am
   alone on the land
When the low sweep of the sunwarmed country
   returns to me like a forgotten dream
I could wish that we had been born as they
To take our day with the essence of laughter
And when the sunset silhouettes the forked elm
   To fall apart amongst the flowers
   Forgotten, forgetting what we should never have known.

[*Winter?* *1938–9*] TS

[8]

What the half-open door said to the empty room

What the half-open door said to the empty room
when a chance draft ruffled the pages of an
old scorebook which happened to be lying
on top of a cupboard when the last
blazer had gone home.

Waft, waft, thou Summer wind,
No blade is so unkind
Of white ribbed Winter's blast:

Thou blow'st, from day to week
Dust upon beauty's cheek
And mak'st them one, at last.

[*Winter? 1938–9*] TS

A meeting – et seq. (2)

Together we stood
On the edge of the world
The sun was like a scimitar
In the hands of a dying Sultan
Together we stood.

I loved you more than I have ever loved before
Either you, or anyone else.
The way you spoke brought tears to my eyes
And I suddenly felt I had done you a great wrong.

And as the sun fell
I left you
And neither of us are dead

But I still remember
When the torn banners of life were for the
    moment furled
And we stood, that summer evening,
Together, on the edge of the world.

[*Winter? 1938–9*] TS

Summer Nocturne

Now night perfumes lie upon the air,
As rests the blossom on the loaded bough;
And each deep-drawn breath is redolent
Of all the folded flowers' mingled scent
That rises in confused rapture now.
As from some cool vase filled with petals rare:
And from the silver goblet of the moon
A ghostly light spills down on arched trees,
And filters through their lace to touch the flowers
Among the grass; the silent, dark moon-hours
Flow past, born on the wayward breeze
That wanders through the quiet night of June.
Now time should stop; the web of charm is spun
By the moon's fingers over lawns and flowers;
All pleasures I would give, if this sweet night
Would ever stay, cooled by the pale moonlight;
But no! for in a few white-misted hours
The East must yellow with to-morrow's sun.

The Coventrian, April 1939 CP

Founder's Day, 1939

(1)

I looked for a pearl
And I found but a stone
I hoped for rose-curl
– Save the wind's moan
And the rain's whirl
I was alone.

I waited a while
And uttered sun-call
Wet pavements smashed tile
Of rose and blue, all;
O, I hoped for your smile
I met a blank wall.

(2)

All day the clouds hung over the cathedral
Like soggy paper bags bursting with water
And spilt their water onto the spire
And along its narrow streets.
All day raindrops spattered against stretched umbrellas
All day I bubbled with curses
While the silly, pointless rain trotted down
Or fell, like a silver sword,
Avenging some old wrong.

Yes, now you can dimly shine and gild the clouds
Now they have departed, now the pavilion is locked
And the wide field empty;
Now no sound breaks the dark whole of the building
As night blocks the tall windows of the silent hall

And the dim eyes of John Hales
Stare into the thickening gloom.

[*Summer 1939*] TS

'This is one of those whiteghosted mornings'

This is one of those whiteghosted mornings
Of early winter, when the sun is red;
Our side of the pane is coldly wet
And every left leaf trembles
With a drop of sun dew,
High, high above
The sky is blue.

The kind of day that burns down to
Bonfires at four o'clock,
And rotten apples on the leafclogged lawn;
The blue smoke drifting across the brickdark road
As the boys come running home from school.

[1939] CHP

'We see the spring breaking across rough stone'

We see the spring breaking across rough stone
    And pause to regard the sky;
But we are pledged to work alone,
    To serve, bow, nor ask if or why.

Summer shimmers over the fishpond.
    We heed it but do not stop
At the may-flies' cloud of mist,
    But penetrate to skeleton beyond.
Autumn is the slow movement;
    We gather our harvest and thank the lofty dusk.
Although glad for the grain, we are
    Aware of the husk.
And winter closes on us like a shroud.
    Whether through windows we shall see spring again
Or not, we are sure to hear the rain
    Chanting its ancient litany, half-aloud.

1939 CHP, CP

'Having grown up in shade of Church and State'

Having grown up in shade of Church and State
    Breathing the air of drawing-rooms and scent,
Following the Test Match, tea unsweet in Lent,
    Been given quite a good bat when aged eight,
With black suit, School House tie, and collar white,
    Two hair-brushes and comb, a curl to coax,
He smiles demurely at his uncle's jokes,
    And reads the *Modern Boy* in bed at night.

And when, upon the cricket field, he bats,
    – All perfect strokes – (one sees the dotted line)
And with a careful twelve tries not to vex,
    We hear the voice: 'Y'know, he's good! Why, that's
A graceful player!' True? Perhaps. Benign,
    We diagnose a case of good old sex.

[*before June 1939*] 1st COL, CHP, CP

Note by Larkin in 1st Collection: 'June 8th. – Pleasant enough day. Cricket –
11 runs. Write two good sonnets at night.' – Author's diary.
l.14 Acknowledgments to Evelyn Waugh.

[16]

The Days of thy Youth

Ah, the rock is crumbling
And our foothold slipping:
Near the horizon there are clouds;
The sun still shines
But the wind, the wind, is rising;
And some have already gone before,
Some will soon go.
But for the second we are safe . . .

Yet under the sun there can be nothing durable,
And you will change, and grow,
And flourish, and, then, toppling, decline;
And very shortly be less than a name
Chipped upon stone, washed by November rains;
Far away, I shall be nothing more.

And nothing will be left to show
Why I am standing here, twisting this cord,
Watching your calm young eyes as you regard
A scene a long way off, as the cold night
Drops veil on veil across the windy skies.

25 June 1939 1st COL, AL 13

Note by Larkin: 'June 25th. – In morning read "Ecclesiastes" – very good – and
write a quite good poem.' – Author's Diary.
l.16. 'this cord': window cord in pavilion.
[A different earlier version was published in *About Larkin* 13, April 2002.]

The Ships at Mylae

You are not happy here. Not here,
When the aching wind sweeps
Or when the rain beats upon the empty streets
Or night moans, and trees toss
Like women in labour.

Not when the world's strings are muted by Snow
Tipping the utmost twigs
Over the dark ice of the pond.

Not when your face is jaded and lined
By electric lights and blotting paper
Not when January darkens at four p.m.
   and the fields are sullen and muddy
   and faces are yellow with artificial light
   and lost cars
   hissing through the
   icy dusk
   actual shroud
   of the wormy winter night
   and the trees
   stand, stuck like
   many strange shapes of iron
   waiting for nothing
   dripping with
   drops of sour rain

   Stanley!
You who serene from unsung argosies
Gazed on the mounting foam!
Feeling the ship bound forward as the rowers
Swept with their oars the full breast of the sea!
Surely you knelt on many a sunwarmed rock

To toss torn flowers into a deep pool
Or let the waves unheeded wash your feet
As expectant you scanned the line
Where blues of skies and seas are wed.
Surely you looked upon an empty world
From some new hill
And the leaping new sun
Made the gold lights of your hair dance
In some lost pagan adoration!
Ran down to an empty beach
And saw the first waves break, and
The first spume fly from the black, unbroken rocks!
Lived every day to the ultimate second
And when at last night fell
Surely you lay calm – breathing under the stars
Dreaming of nothing but the unanalysed sweetness of
life.

    8 July 1939 1st COL

Note by Larkin: 'July 8th. – At night write poetry. "Ships at Mylae": I think fair. Good idea badly worked out.' – Diary.
The title, and the inspiration of the whole poem, came from a line in Eliot's *The Waste Land*: 'Stetson!/You who were with me in the ships at Mylae!' The line is incorporated thus: 'Stanley!/You who serene, &c.'

Alvis Victrix

What is this voluptuous monster, painted red,
Silently swimming along the Albany Road
With flabby lecher with a paunch well-fed,
Steering home to some rich-hung abode?
Regard his lips, like fat pink coffin-worms,
His padded hands that idly twist the wheel;
His puffy eyes are like malignant germs,
And obscene glances covertly do steal.

But see the rose on the rich, rotting heap;
The golden hair, the close-hugged cricket cap,
The folded flannels, and the oiled bat,
Eyes as calm as summer seas in sleep,
White hands neat folded on the docile lap,
Sitting, bolt upright, on the cushions fat.

12 July 1939 1st COL

Note by Larkin: 'The poem was conceived July 11th, and written July 12th. The version here is inferior to one sent to F. G. Smith, but is the original in all but one word.'

Stanley en Musique

The dull whole of the drawing room
Is crucified with crystal nails,
Dresden shepherdesses smirk
As Stanley practises his scales;

Maternal corsets creak delight
At faultless sequence from beneath;
Brows furrowed at his taxing task
His tongue peeps out between his teeth;

(He tops the uniformity
of natal avenue; his tie
is knotted neat, and penny cards
put Sunday wrinkles round his eye)

The rhythm breaks, and then reforms
Into bowel-piercing waltz supreme:
His washed hands trace the melody
Of 'When I grow Too Old to Dream'.

Th'adjusted clock upon the shelf
Tells him of his hour the end;
The lid he closes, and slips off
To   with a friend.

15 July 1939 1st COL

Note by Larkin: 'July 15th. – At night type out "Alvis Victrix" and write
"Stanley en Musique". Eliotian but amusing. Somehow, one can't be serious
about Sanders. He is too – how shall I put it? Oh, I don't know.' – Diary.
l.16: This line, although complete in the original, still awaits satisfactory
completion.
Note by Larkin on the following page: '(The next of the Stanley poems was
"Stanley à tatons". It was the first effort at serious writing on this subject, and
is not included here partly because it is a bad poem, and partly because it is
untrue. But the diary comment ran: "He has now become Adolescence to me–
pre-natal, I mean." This is a decided link between the earlier poems and the
later ones.)'
['Stanley' was evidently Larkin's schoolfriend, Earnest Stanley Saunders.]

Street Lamps

When night slinks, like a puma, down the sky,
  And the bare, windy streets echo with silence,
Street lamps come out, and lean at corners, awry,
  Casting black shadows, oblique and intense;
So they burn on, impersonal, through the night,
  Hearing the hours slowly topple past
Like cold drops from a glistening stalactite,
  Until grey planes splinter the gloom at last;
Then they go out.

            I think I noticed once
  – T'was morning – one sole street-lamp still bright-lit
Which, with a senile grin, like an old dunce,
  Vied the blue sky, and tried to rival it;
  And, leering pallid though its use was done,
Tried to cast shadows contrary to the sun.

The Coventrian, September 1939 CP

'When the night puts twenty veils'

When the night puts twenty veils
Over the sun, and the west sky pales
   To black its vast sweep:
   Then all is deep
Save where the street lamp gleams upon the rails.

This summertime must be forgot
– It will be, if we would or not –
   Who lost or won?
   Oblivious run:
And sunlight, if it could, would coldly rot.

So. Let me accept the role, and call
Myself the circumstances' tennis-ball:
   We'll bounce: together
   Or not, whether
Either, let no tears silent fall.

[*before September 1939*] CHP, CP

[23]

À un ami qui aime

Disparaging my taste in ties
    Relaxed warmly on my lap,
I gazed into his lovely eyes
    And saw the snow beyond the gap.

    I could elaborate this theme
        But think that I shall not;
    If one can accept the dream
        The rest is best forgot.

    For everywhere the traps are laid;
        We must remember blooms,
    And pianos being played
        In sunlit morning rooms,

For life is not a storm of love,
    Nor a tragedy of sex:
It only is a question of
    Deriving joy from shapely necks.

[*September–October 1939*] TS, AL 13

'The grinding halt of plant, and clicking stiles'

The grinding halt of plant, and clicking stiles,
Releases on the streets a second horde
Cleaned from steel-chipped sweat: cool and new
Yet with an aching in the legs and feet
Which cheats a Grecian holiday.
Feet slabbily resound on pavement stones,
Silk mufflers are touched by slanting rays
From the west, where the burnt sun sinks.

The old procession of the sexual march
10   Leads o'er familiar ways. The urined trees,
The horse's oval stain, the canine filth,
The horde of houses under the sapphire sky
Crouching aggressively in their dirt –
We know it. Dabs of black and white
Lead weary feet to littered carpet-tufts
Hearsall Common waits, a broken charger.

A young, dishonoured hand seeks iron support
– We have not captured Ratisbon, and so
Naturally, anything in the nature of a death
20   Is not involved – creeping beneath the blue
Of sleeve, the threaded device, the hand; seeking
The opal balloon again, eyes spin: trees, trousers
Cigarette paper, and the memory
Of soggy sandbags topsy like a spun mirror.

Eight hours . . . the white, thick coffee cup,
Descending crumbs like parachutes: the eyes,
Incurious, inquiring . . . for the hundredth time
He straightens the absurd cap, thrilling as
His fingers touch the alien serge and badge.
30   Even yet, the novelty is fresh unwrapped,

And crisp hair palpitates
In biscuit curls.

Minutes hop away like fleas, and as small;
The block-square action of a charted force
Admits no weakness in its mortared bricks;
Ankles touch above black polished shoes
Knees, elbows pressing, holding . . .
'Hold, hold, hold . . . Jesus hung in night,
There was mud in the trenches, and strength
40   In the War Office telegram. . . .'

'Land of Hope and Glory' on a crakt whistle
Stimulates adrenalin. Perform a duty:
Snap of a salute: the smiles, lined,
The boiled smile,
The indifferent corner of a dry moustache.
At last the hand reaches the hour: Withdraw!
Disperse your troops, slacken shoulders, knees
Aching with the promise of cushions and horsehair.

A splintered day reforms under the evening sky;
50   The whistled tune clips a frayed edge as
At the corner of a street (which might be
The edge of the world) one is conscious
Of a fluid body underneath the uniform;
Between the absurd tilt and the stiff collar
Moves a book, a poem, a symphony
In creation, not yet formed and finished.

The lamp post fits the shoulders for a minute;
The cavernous depth of a news-sellers [sic] mouth
Announces victory (price one penny).
60   Away the opal balloon sways at its cable.
With grass-sweeping roar the bomber's wheels lift
And surge into the sun, away into the west,

[26]

Where the last rays glint on the wing,
And the illusive spinning disc, and the snouted bombs.

He who has never felt the sunlit wall,
Or the dust kicked by a cricket boot;
Walked husk-like amongst the sunshaded parents
Flowered around the mown grass where the shadows
Lengthen as the sun declines over the pavilion –
70   He longs, in the movement of an eyebrow,
To fly away himself, into the heat of noon
Leaving the dewy grass where he now stands;

The same hand that leant against a wheel
Would seize the gear of life, and clash the cogs,
To rise into the upper air, distending
Hair-lined nostrils to the acid stratosphere,
Kept from some eyes by spectacles. Alas!
A cockpit glance shows the warm summer land
Left behind, voluntarily, left, left, never
80   To revisit . . . But impatience stands:

The unblown trumpet wakes the dormant heart:
Hints of pipes, and control
Of bigger and larger and oilier and noisier
Machines: (poison for clear skin, opium for eyes,
Dullness for hair, blotting paper to life's elixir
As the years pad over) But enlarge the shoes!
Abolish sub-elevation! Cast the cap
Into the shadow of the motor bike!

Words stumble: stay awhile, could you not
90   Watch, with us, one hour? We, to whom
The quivering sprig, dew-flicked [sic], against blue
And wool-white is life, we urge
That your hand should not shadow the paternal watch
Before your time; let the sunlight weave your hair,

Before it is matted by a hat; let your lips laugh
Before they take the shredding cigarette . . .

As shadows of lamp posts tell us time fades
With outstretched hands we leave the retreating back
And hear the echo of the shining feet
Treading the kiss with uncomprehending eyes . . .
A body nerved with ambition to suicide.

100

[*September–October 1939*] TS (line numbering is in TS)

[28]

'Smash all the mirrors in your home'

Smash all the mirrors in your home,
Don't look at blinded shop windows;
Wear wrong clothes, read authors you dislike;
Sleep in the rain, ask twenty different people
The way to your own house; clean your bike;
Scrub your scullery; translate eighty Latin
Lines a day; learn Greek;
Brush up your German.

Walking, note light on a factory,
Worn shoes in a window, old records,
The great meat, and the poulterer gutting a rabbit,
The shine from new Cornish pasties.
Here coats hang, the Jew blinks in a doorway,
Posters flap victory receding dropping rewards,
And the autumn leaves
Sweep driven over the railway.

Talking, watching, see the man's hands,
Woman's head turning, child absorbed in nothing.
Take friends not as extensions, but people.
See the dog-pulled, mask biblike, who is he?
The blimpish woman, purple and powdered,
Nature's whore, say you, so what, say I?
And whom you love, make comfortable with
    cushions,
Make tea, conversation, but don't beg.

Love. – Get it, narrow beam to burning dot
White and intense, intensify, then
Spread the focus, see all as they are,
All faces as white, minds as scrolls.
Feed love fires intellect, till the cold blaze

Splits shell, cracks cocoon, lights the new page
Ready for sharpened pencil; lose life
In the great light of the waiting souls.

[*September–October 1939*] TS

'Watch, my dear, the darkness now'

Watch, my dear, the darkness now
Poured around the chimney pots
Velvetly upon your hair
Pale where autumn sunlight sets
Softening collisions raw
That are part of day's set pace
Mending now the rend and tear
Of light's brambles. Now remains
Only leaves' whisk over stones
And the starlight on your face.

Maudlin sensuality
Possibly is cause of this
But the unlived life awaits
Falls behind us as we pass
Sense's sole reality
Tells me of your lovely mouth
All the various loves and hates
Mingle to a single phrase
'Run the night until its close.
Fight before all life is south.'

[*September–October 1939*] TS

'Turning from obscene verses to the stars'

Turning from obscene verses to the stars
The bells remind us of the sleeping roofs,
   The coming hostile stares,
    And serried graves.

Diversity protests too much, methinks.
Yet others looked, and they found as few keys . . .
   We accept them with some thanks,
    But they don't help the days.

One is tempted strongly to accept
The individual reality
   World, in hung flesh lapt,
    The past, a nullity.

But O, diversity is preferable to that!
The ever-vicious circle of green horror,
   The filter for the lot
    And the eternal mirror!

And now the clock has struck the quarter-hour.
I have a feeling that I don't like life;
   But life likes me, and draws me near
    Her shining teeth.

[*September–October 1939*] VOH (The last four lines are quoted in
a letter to J. B. Sutton, 31 October 1945.)

'Lock the door, Lariston, lock it, I say to you'

(from James Hogg)

Lock the door, Lariston, lock it, I say to you,
Latch it and lock it and look from the pane:
   There, you see, in the bushes?
   The obvious hushes –
They are beginning to watch you again.

O, watch the west, Lariston, 'way on the whitening
Road gleams the glitter of gasbomb and gun;
   They have been plotting
   Compulsory rotting,
To saw up the moon, and to blow out the sun.

O, lock the door, Lariston, laughing is madness now,
Leap from your ingle-nook, no time to cringe,
   Lock it, don't vacillate –
   No, it is now too late.
They are here, and have splintered it straight from the
   hinge.

[*September–October 1939*] VOH

'Has all history rolled to bring us here?'

Has all history rolled to bring us here?
If so, it needn't interfere;
Further rolling will suit us fine.
(We lit the last fire with the warning sign)
There's nothing to do any more. All the lights are out.

It's not worth the trouble, nor the expense;
Out in the park, a rotting fence
Falls to the weeds; in the woods there are spies
Watching the windows with their great big eyes.
There's nothing to do any more. All the lights are out.

They've blocked the roads to the hills, and now
We can't get away if we wanted to.
The servants have gone, I expect, out of a back way;
We sit here watching the shut of day.
There's nothing to do any more. All the lights are out.

The floor is littered with odds and ends
Half-smoked cigarettes, photos of friends;
In the butler's pantry the mice now lurk;
And the piano keys are stiff and won't work.
There's nothing to do any more. All the lights are out.

The bottle now is nearly done:
There isn't even enough for one.
Better leave it for he who will find
The rumpled sofa and the hand behind.
There's nothing to do any more. All the lights are out.

[*September–October 1939*] TS

[34]

'In a second I knew it was your voice speaking'

In a second I knew it was your voice speaking
Caught along the wind
For a second I lived through the summer weeks
And others, sometimes finding
What I had hoped for, what I thought
With heart and mind.

Yet as I trod on, my feet stamped out the burning
Flame sprung in me
My heart sobbed, cried 'O go back! Return!
What is the use of fleeing?'
But on, on: the rain thrust you behind again
Cried: To be.

[*September–October 1939*] TS

A study in light and dark

The glow, back over the common, comes from
    the railway:
that's the Church candle, been burning now
    quite a number of years:
there, that's the light the lover flicks
as he follows the joys of consummation with
    the joys of a cigarette:
that light was the flash as a man shot himself:
that's a searchlight feeling for bombers:
there, the light appears as the squinting
    wife regards the fuddled husband:
these are twin headlights of a capitalist's car:
this, the gaslight of a trodden worker who
    would tread:
that's the light of a cinema:
that's the light of Mars
that's the moon
that's a match

    Alone now, in my dark room,
    The pebbles cease to drop into the rocking pool
    And gradually the surface quietens
    Reflecting image of darkest peace and silence.
    No questions catch the clothes
    But only as it were a spreading
    Draws all threads to their finished pattern
    And you are pieced together bit by bit
    Set against the evening
    Lovely and glowing, like a chain of gold.

[*September–October 1939*] TS

'Autumn sees the sun low in the sky'

Autumn sees the sun low in the sky;
Leans gently, washing the pale landscape,
   With long shadows;
When the berries hang in the hedges
The sun softly freckles the lanes
   And lights the meadows.

On a late, pale blue afternoon
Thought, as my shadow gesticulated before me
   On sunlit tuft,
How like all the evenings in summer it was,
When we held the same cup in unrelated hands,
   And drank the same draught.

[*September–October 1939*] TS (as 'Autumn Refrain'), VOH

[37]

'Within, a voice said: Cry!'

Within, a voice said: Cry!
Your sorrow will become
Less, if you fashion some
Half-thought into half-lie.

But without, the soiled mesh
Of clouds on sun shines gold
Upon the metal cold
Of leaves, polished afresh.

Without, O, somewhere,
Not knowing who or where
I am, or how despair
Gnaws at my life anew.

[*September–October 1939*] ts

'What is the difference between December and January?'

What is the difference between December and January?
Between green December and frosty January
between frosty December and sunny January
What is it?

December is the brick wall bruising apples
the final clamp on the aching mist
the deepening of red to black
the last log before the windows pale.

December says: last laughter
last laughter before hail is met
last laughter before you shut the door behind you
Feel shapes of dead trees in wind and rain.

January is black
There, frozen out of movement, fingers can't find
fields scalloped in black iron
heart held by aching iron.

January says: first aching
first aching when holed bucket is half ice-held
first aching when calendar leaves are crushed
in remembered dates.

The difference lies under the snow
in the black tree boles
what they were, what are, are becoming:
Death has claimed, and the march goes on.

[*September–October 1939*] TS

'Falling of these early flowers'

Falling of these early flowers
Under winter clouds of rain
Rends the lover's heart;
Yet the wind that wrecks the shrine
And the rotting of the stairs
Should be a deeper death.
Pull of mind from form apart
Will for ever sing the seas;
The constant thought, behind the eyes
That change at every breath.

Fading of this early flower,
As the turning suns deride,
Whispers now at evening:
'Everything falls to the shade,
Gasping to the withered air,
Once was beautiful.'
Impervious to reasoning,
The frantic answer dies alike:
'O what need have you thus to take.
Who is so wonderful?'

[*September–October 1939*] TS, VOH

To a friend's acquaintance

Are you my innocent? I expect you are:
   Still, it doesn't matter;
Remote as even the nearest star
   That I see flutter
   In the pool, in the gutter.

(These aren't my first words to you; I
   Did write many
More, further back, under quite a different sky –
   Words like honey.
   Sickly and sunny.)

But you may as well be accepted as the
   Latest in ideals;
(New model for my troops) a divinity
   Dead as all grails
   When the defence fails.

[*September–October 1939*] TS

To a friend

O let the passing moon delight
To touch the pillow where you lie,
And let her cool hand smooth away
All hint of mortality,
Awareness of a coming fate,
And every other trace of stress:
Let the settling night obey.
When at last the windows shine,
Stirred by opal clouds of dawn
May you rise in loveliness.

In the nightmare of the years,
And the torment of the hours,
May the summer rest on you
With a trace of former flowers,
As the evening breeze repairs
Rakings of a years repass;
And the kiss that stays as true
Bring to you instinctive peace,
Something of a careless grace
That rests upon the summer grass.

[*September–October 1939*] TS, AL 13

Note: This TS has notations by Larkin that may have been made at the time he
went through these poems to prepare The Village of the Heart – or they may
be earlier. They do not permit the construction of a corrected version. The
word 'years' for 'year' in line 16 was probably a typing error.

A farewell

Take your tomorrow: go, I give you leave
    To turn your face from me;
Yet ask that you should save
One backward look, as at the door you stand,
To sign my love, before your hand
    Floods the sun's ecstasy.

That I might think you knew your power
    Which takes you now from me,
And know why as you go I must stay here.
For you are born to triumph; I decay,
And as you turn to take your waiting day,
    Remain in atrophy.

[*September–October 1939*] TS

[43]

Young Woman Blues

So if you saw him not alone
But living, in that distant land,
Then all my life is overthrown
   All days
   Are vain:
Yet if I weep now, who will understand?

O there can be no second love
For me; go, soldier, to your wars;
I shall remain, the hills to rove,
   And stay
   Away
Letting the cold night cover me with stars.

[*September–October 1939*] TS

[44]

'Lie there, my tumbled thoughts'

Lie there, my tumbled thoughts,
That through th'involuntary year
Have fallen hot without retorts;
   Queer
Medley now, of loves,
And daily hate, and yearly fear,
Of the mind taking off its gloves,
   Into nudity, sheer.

So we are encrusted
With the days, bright interlocked,
And learn that only time is trusted.
   Pistol cocked
We pass through knotted jungle
Ready to be shot, or shocked,
And find, alert for private bungle,
   Coffins, inscribed, unlocked.

[*September–October 1939*] TS

'Now the shadows that fall from the hills'

Now the shadows that fall from the hills
Darken the walls: all the meadows
Sleep under their trees: and distant the stars
Stretch far beyond, to spin, to freeze.

So the pull of memory only makes me grasp,
Standing here, where we so often stood,
How you, and others, are the trees and fields,
Near; and I, more distant that [sic] I ever knew.

[*September–October 1939*] ts

'The pistol now again is raised'

The pistol now again is raised
   The ruler poised to draw the line
The final letter is ready phrased
   And waits the sign
   But there's no sign.

For something scuttles from the shade
   New mood chases mood half gone
Laugh at scene painstakingly laid
   And pass on
   Clock ticks on.

Have seen you for the last time now
   Several times at least. The drums
Drive the dying army through the snow
   And the laugh comes
   And spring comes.

One day darkness will drag us down
   Fall faintly, glad of its powerful blow
Apart, we are old, a day older, we drown
   And the hours grow
   And the crops grow.

[*September–October 1939*] TS

'Praise to the higher organisms!'

Praise to the higher organisms!
   Aristocrats
Impervious to private prisms
And the new moon in glass.
O, let us kneel at their cheap pointed feet,
And then retreat.

Those to whom analysis
   Is foreign,
Such indecency as this
Silly as D. H. Lawrence;
O come, let us drink with sewage of reality
To true morality.

And, especially, the Kings
   Be remembered;
To whom life is coloured rings,
   Violin's ecstasies, leaves in September.
May their deaths be amusing as old steeples
And other people's.

[*September–October 1939*] TS, VOH

[48]

'The hills in their recumbent postures'

The hills in their recumbent postures
  Look into the silent lake;
The bare trees stare across the pastures,
  Waiting for the wind to wake.

As evening dims these sculptured forms
  The mind demands of mortal eye:
'If one should fall among these farms,
  Would not the lake reflect the sky?'

[*September–October 1939*] TS (as 'Homage to Daddy
Lamartine'), VOH, CHP, CP

[49]

Stanley et la Glace

Three pennies gain a twisted whorl
Of cold ice-cream, coiled in a wreath;
I, fascinated, watch your tongue
Curl pink beyond your little ivory teeth.

Lap, lap . . . just as, perhaps, a cat
With planted paws and bended head
Would flick the surface of its milk
Vibrating purrs when it at last felt fed . . .

But these Homeric similes
Inadequately fail to say
How, even though you were a tongue
Your eyes watched moving forms, shapes, faraway;

Although the fibres of your frame
Were concentrated, pink and small,
Not even the ice-cream could claim
To occupy you, brain and eyes and all.

We, who adore you, can but serve.
We lay no claim to be your guide;
Merely husks of coiled ice-cream
Who have come this far, happy, at your side.

14 September 1939 1st COL

Note by Larkin: 'Sept. 14th. – Write "Stanley et la Glace". Not very
good.' – Diary.

Erotic Play

Your summer will sing of this.
  – I know it, (if it sings at all);
Quand vous serez bien vieux . . .
  Memories of sunlit wall;

Golden hours of broken talk
  'Neath the crab-backed apple tree;
Friends far scattered, factory-side;
  Home and sisters – even me?

Do I grudge your wasted hours
  When my own flow like a tide
Of ice-grey misery, or else
  Golden, when I'm at your side?

When you enjoy your scattered time
  Who am I to question you?
You are merely doing that
  Which is more than I can do.

19 September 1939 1st COL

Note by Larkin: 'Sept. 19th. – Morning, another episode of "Erotic Play"
(I write a poem called this).' – Diary.
l.3 cf. Ronsard.

'Autumn has caught us in our summer wear'

Autumn has caught us in our summer wear
  Brother, and the day
  Breathes coldly from fields far away
  As white air.
We are cold at our feet, and cold at our throats,
Crouching, cold, deaf to the morning's half-notes.

See, over the fields are coming the girls from the Church,
  Gathering the fruits
  For their Harvest Festival; leaves, berries and roots
  – Such is their search.
I do not think that we shall be
Troubled by their piety.

Tomorrow we shall hear their old bells ringing
  For another year;
  We shall achingcold be here
  – Not singing.
Outside, the frost will bite, thaw, then return;
Inside, the candle will burn.

[*late 1939*] CHP, CP

Evensong

'I think I read, or have been told,
    That once there was a thing called love;
(The pages of the manuscripts
    Give lyrics to a lady's glove).

'Today we pace the sexual stones
    And coyish shrieks we cutely utter;
Sexual laughter rings along
    The cynic echo of the gutter.

'The empty faces drip delight,
    The scabrous hands grope for a mate,
Happy in imbecility
    Our mental age is roughly eight.

'But who am I to curse or carp?
    I, fashioned with a face that's odd?
For every wise man's son doth know,
    The people's voice is that of God.'

[*late 1939?*] (letter to J. B. Sutton) TS

[53]

'Why did I dream of you last night?'

Why did I dream of you last night?
Now morning is pushing back hair with grey light
Memories strike home, like slaps in the face:
Raised on elbow, I stare at the pale fog beyond the window.

So many things I had thought forgotten
Return to my mind with stranger pain:
– Like letters that arrive addressed to someone
Who left the house so many years ago.

[1939] CHP, CP

Chorus from a Masque

You take our advice
If life isn't nice
The fault's with you;
Points of view
Reveal that some
Are happy, handsome,
Rich, or carefree:
You're contrary
You are the misfit
All along
Though you don't think it
You are wrong.

[*1939?*] (originally in 'Behind the Facade')
PAug40, CHP

Holograph note by Larkin in Poems August 1940: 'This is a year earlier than the other shit . . .'

Prologue

Such is our springtime, sprawling its sprouting
Leaves to the laughing of flat gramophones
  But it cannot deceive
  Or even save
  Who sardonically greet
  The simple and great.

[*before April 1940*] VOH

'Prince, fortune is accepted among these rooms'

Prince, fortune is accepted among these rooms
That have echoes when lit vith voices
    Of the unbruised that roam
    Caressive under our shadowing vices:

Awaiting when they can assume the coming
Life. In the meantime the names attest
    So many delicious identities skimming
    Each unknown and unloving artist

That parades unconscious to our leprous eyes
Loved but forgetful of the claiming hearth,
    Attaining, unsusceptible to ease,
    Like a king his earth.

[*before April 1940*] VOH, CHP

[57]

'Standing on love's farther shores'

Standing on love's farther shores
   He reflects:
Wonders at his memory of tears,
Letters unposted; remembered facts
Forming the pattern of a well-known tale
In which he made moves, was checked,
   And left the table.

So on the cooler banks
   He stands;
Through that flood of fire, thinks,
I fought; watches where its rage extends,
Considers who and how he was;
Yet crossing leaves, from other lands,
   No mark nor traces.

[*before April 1940*] VOH

[58]

'The cycles hiss on the road away from the factory'

The cycles hiss on the road away from the factory
Bearing their lights through the dark: the old man knows
He will take his leather bag from the handlebars;
The youth swing into the lighted kitchen: the journey
    Complete, the boy recognise the childhood doors.

In the deeper city, among the thunder of buses,
The laughter of standing youths drowns the cry
Of the news-seller with his eternal today.
And at warm theatre doors some are showing their passes
    Ignorant of neurotic schoolgirls in the library.

Multiplication of examples is not needed
To show the individual vibrations of the chord
That is this night. Yet only the normal lover's jarred
Mind feels its grief. For other's worth is graded,
    And in an hour some will have died.

8 February 1940 VOH

'So you have been, despite parental ban'

So you have been, despite parental ban
   That would not hear the old demand again;
One who through rain to empty station ran
   And bought a ticket for the early train.

We heard of all your gain when you had gone,
   And talked about it when the meal lay done,
The night drawn in, electric light switched on,
   Your name breathed round the tealeaves and last bun:

How you had laughed, the night before you left;
   All your potentialities, untried,
Their weakness doffed, became our hero, deft,
   The don, the climber on the mountain side:

We knew all this absurd, yet were not sad.
   Today your journey home is nearly done:
That bag above your head, the one you had
   When seventeen, when you were still a son,

Is labelled now with names we do not know;
   The gloved hands hang between the static knees,
And show no glee at closing evening's glow –
   Are you possessor of the sought-for ease?

That name for which you fought – does it quite fit?
   And is your stubborn silence only tact?
Boys wish to imitate who hear of it –
   But will you tell them to repeat your act?

16 March 1940 (date from 'Intellectual Diary') VOH, CHP, CP

[60]

'Through darkness of sowing'

Through darkness of sowing
And hours of saying
That such is not dead
Or believing in glowing
You as a braid
Bright, run as a thread;
In these moments of seeing
Our eyes meet from turning
You from your leisure
I from life's fading
– Meet in the censure
Of the sun's pleasure.

Then all my training
Argues in rising
To break down your bluff:
But the great simple singing
Of you, as a leaf,
Or your personal laugh
Silences question.
    You are the reason
    From reason unwrapped
    That exists without caution
    Gold none can corrupt
    And all must accept.

18 March 1940 (date from 'Intellectual Diary')
VOH, CHP

[61]

'Nothing significant was really said'

Nothing significant was really said,
Though all agreed the talk superb, and that
The brilliant freshman with his subtle thought
Deserved the praise he won from every side.
All but one declared his future great,
His present sure and happy; they that stayed
Behind, among the ashes, were all stirred
By memory of his words, as sharp as grit.

The one had watched the talk: remembered how
He'd found the genius crying when alone;
Recalled his words: 'O what unlucky streak
Twisting inside me, made me break the line?
What was the rock my gliding childhood struck,
And what bright unreal path has led me here?'

18 March 1940 (date from 'Intellectual Diary') VOH, CHP, CP

Epilogue

Will hoped-for rains
Bring our delight
   And springing profit?
Or will six sterile Junes
Kill: or worse, the bright
   Giant obliterate?

[*before April 1940*] VOH, CHP

Spring Warning

And the walker sees the sunlit battlefield
Where winter was fought: the broken sticks in the
    sun:
        Allotments fresh spaded: here are seen
        The builders on their high scaffold,
            And the red clubhouse flag.
The light, the turf, and all that grows now urge
The uncertain dweller blinking to emerge,
To learn the simpler movements of the jig
And free his gladder impulses from gag.

But there are some who mutter: 'Joy
Is for the simple or the great to feel,
        Neither of which we are.' They file
        The easy chain that bound us, jeer
            At our ancestral forge:
Refuse the sun that flashes from their high
Attic windows, and follow with their eye
The muffled boy, with his compelling badge,
On his serious errand riding to the gorge.

The Coventrian, April 1940 CP

Long Jump

This rectangle cut
From our green field
Has the appearance of a grave,
And we as mourners move
Or stand beside
It in a shuffling knot.
Strange, o strange the picture!
From railings where errandboys lean
Below green budding trees
To the scattered entrants with bare arms and knees
In everything a unity of line
A momentary perfect structure
Centred on jumper flashing past blurred faces
Scattering flurried earth:
Design extended to the little watching crowds
And the cathedrals of bright flying clouds
Across the earth and us, speaking of death.

So strange that these appreciative gazes
Of the few awkward watchers might provoke
A question as to motives and intent:
'Is it a boredom, friendship, love or loyalty
To half-remembered names holds you in fealty
On this high field: by what far worship sent?
Is there a prayer beneath your anxious joke
For a new earth, a sailing life
Controlled by swinging tides of blood
This scene a glimpse of green to burst the husk?'
And to the shivering boys I longed to ask:
'Whether your mind approves as good or bad,
Paints different colours love and strife,
Tenderness or hate,
Puts reason on desire, your presence here

Might be significant, for, barring fiction,
Is attacking or defence your cause for action?'

Instead, I wandered where
Young men with parted hair contested at
The discus-throwing, and thought how
Spontaneity seemed exiled to this corner
Of fenced school field, acted in derision:
And silently, in words of indecision,
Confirmed how we were all one sneering mourner
Mourning the past in a decaying now:

What beauty there is here is stroked by rot
Mouths speak with a reek of decay
Eyes stare as through water at
The latest circumlocutions of art,
And we, beneath a sky of neutral grey,
Suggest that it is dawn, but fancy not.

But as to the real truth, who knows? The earth
May yet bring forth, the past the future
Flowering over walls, a leaping urge
And I, composer of life's dirge,
Be called upon to broadcast and to nurture,
Assist, not at a funeral, but a birth.

[21 April 1940] TS

Remark

Seconds of tangled love and art,
The mistress-motif, cause the heart
To struggle at its nets;
Conspicuous the urge once more
To clarify and to adore
What nature forward sets.

For as the common joke is love,
The April trick sent from above,
And art a troubling visit –
Their joining in a heart of oak –
Or even deal – makes nature's joke
Unusually exquisite.

[*10 April 1940*] (date from 'Intellectual Diary') FP

[67]

Poem: Study in Four Parts

The poet has a straight face
Otherwise he would be out of place,
Nothing like comedy
Can ever be admitted as poetry.

I

When so many dropped on the harsh
Morning between our century's two nights
Have died like a rag on a nail, with uncrossed hands,
Which of the death-saddened ears will note
A single body's achievement of nineteen years?

The tale is a country one,
Slow as a root for the telling,
How, hatched and thatched,
One difficult day a sleep-walking child
Woke in the house of mirrors,

Saw its name signed
As receiving a load of years; saw the new oil
In the new engines getting greater power;
Saw with a start
Its interesting face, and the faces of all the others.

And in wondering evening walks
The world flew past, and was complete
And catalogued under glass:
And some faces were so beautiful
That their simple images grew wet with tears.

But the mirrors broke and slid
Silver like scales to the ground
And the wind threw the fences down

And the path all eaten with flowers
Strayed into the wood and was lost;

Now vanishing into the hill
The columns of marching men
Are thicker and brighter than wheat,
While under the spread of the moon
The cities lie ruined and mad[?].

II

Now every promise is withdrawn,
And every spring runs underground;
Here are the paths no longer worn
And not a signpost to be found;
   In body and in mind
   The hero stands alone.

The twisted jumbled with the straight,
The years are telescoped and burnt;
Much will never be retaught
Now, that we have never learnt;
   All unprepared are sent
   Against the failing light.

Dumb among the rocks and sand
Prayers are waiting to be said;
Prayers will never understand
What's left of the prayerless dead –
   Blood beating in my hand
   Words climbing in my head.

III

Yet I do not want to end
With a night falling and the wind and no stars

[69]

And, faintly, the high-flying bombers:
The years push each other away
And rooms and their faces recede,
And I will build no tomb on your day
Any more than travellers consecrate a house
Where they were warm and happy for a night.

I will blow these words through no trumpet,
Coil after coil of metal praise;
Unfurl no figured banner to the wind
To be saluted by the grave cadets
And sold on ashtrays at a monument;
Tonight, hands in my pockets,
I face the window to Wales, and merely stare
In your wet direction.

For the time of heroics is past,
Farther than our forgotten childhoods,
Those acid summers of the twenties
When Lawrence still saw hope for some of us,
But died before the thirties stamped it out;
Now there is nothing left to swear or promise,
No everlasting past or future;
Only this day in a nameless town.

And my thoughts tracking the empty roads
To your nameless town, where you
Will be sitting with your hands across your knees
Smiling at another sealed-up year
Dropped like a sun behind suburban houses;
Flushed and timid are the kindnesses
And wanting the old unnoticed life again,
The clocks put back and winter coming on.

So I lift a dark glass
Fluent against the light,

And soft as a licking candle say my wish;
Over the wine of memory and hoping,
Soft as a flame.
Licking the bud of blood and wine, repeat
A rote of prayer for you and yours
On this, your day in the year.

May out of the clouds of chance
A calm wind blow, a bird be sighted and steer
Straight for your bough, and its pursuing love
Break in the air, a scarlet target afloat
For the strength of your striking arrow;
The length of your heart
Be furrowed under your hand,
And the summer's end fall heavy in your arms.

IV

The land in the sun and shadow
And the horns of morning
    Blowing, shining,
Waken the drowned girl
Frosted under the soil
In a dazzling meadow.

For today the flag is flown
From the castle of leaves
    That lives, that lives;
Now will the heir regain
Ten valleys curving in
The chest of the sun;

And loud in the lighted ear
A human year of life
    Is beating in a laugh,
And the sound of silver blood

Bursts in a wave, to flood
A human shore.

[*23 April 1940?*]

Note: In the 'Intellectual Diary' kept by Larkin at this time, he notes: 'April 23rd Type out "Poem" "Study in 4 parts" '. The above poem might be the poem, as it contains the line 'A single body's achievement of nineteen years'. However, on 9 May in the diary he lists the verses that he likes from 'Study in Four Parts', and the number of verses listed is not in keeping with the form of the above poem. The text has many MS alterations.

Hard Lines, or Mean Old W. H. Thomas Blues

Divided by wet roads the fields are wet
With Brown March sucking at the schoolboys' foot;
And apathetic through this afternoon
Of ivied houses barren in the rain
I sit and send my swan of music out.

Barren the lilt of comfort she can salvage
And lost the phrase embroidered on the badge:
The wall-high thinker round the garden shed
Cannot with these go easily to bed
Nor once more melt his year-long thoughts to rage,

Lacking the wordy bloodstream at command,
The green selfconscious spurt that drives the hand
Of Dylan in his womb of whiskey [sic] rocked,
And lacking too the brilliant-muscled tact
Of Auden riding through his ogreland,

Is forced to pause and wonder what it means,
Condemned to blued frenchwindows while it rains,
The slab of garden differing so much
From college lawns mown shaven to the touch
And speaking clock from far friends' conversations.

The same perplexing as the weathers halt
Ready to swamp with summer every fault
That logic winter by a bare gasfire
Has given time and reason to inquire
For every man with fear enough to doubt.

Blank on, dumb river and the bleaching sky,
Cunning behind the trees for all to see,
You show no answers but you keep us taped

[73]

With evidence that cannot well be faked
To make each surgeon like a sinner cry:

'Where does the power come from? Who hears it call?
Are all the chosen chosen when at school?
If they neglect their orders, are they marked
With cancer's swiftly-disappearing tact,
Or do they rot like apples where they fall?'

Some hear the answers in a sexy dorm
Or after summer windy on the prom
Or now as I await a letter's flop
To plait my ragged ends to formal shape
All these and others to the listening come;

For flanked though many be with loaves and wine
An orchardbosomed lover soft as skin
The mastering moments never speak to two
But choose them single as diseases do
And make their books and carpets leave them lone . . .

*

I miss the bull of truth; a raw recruit
Spatter her regions with my stammered set
Of explorations in her provinces
And watch, the shadow of the sun advances
The cold that keeps the summer's flood to cut

Ready to wash and revel all the brain,
Showing the hands the way to love again.
Waxed summer shall burn fierce again this year.
Who is the faceless reaper that I fear?
Where have those visions gone I said I'd seen?

[1940?] TS

[74]

'Quests are numerous; for the far acrid strand'

Quests are numerous; for the far acrid strand
Invites, over the dimpled sea as blue
    As the vast empty sky regarded
    Through hourglass and shifting sand;

Easy, the heraldic clouds
Curled like breath from the fiery
    Nostrils of the sun's horses,
    To watch the horizon,

Seeing there the mirage of desires
Its minarets and lions, through
    The limited telescope
    Of a prejudice or a love.

But easy to remain inert
Watching the whole scene from the sheltered beach
    Under the sun, swinging its arc above
    The tall palm trees,

Until the falling of glass waves, the cry
Of birds merge like blurred angry sun
    Beneath the bloodred eyes, and
    No more is heard, or believed, seen.

4 May 1940 CHP

'For the mind to betray'

For the mind to betray
With its deadly paralytic ray
The unwary body, that is a

Familiar thing. But threnody
Of being sung by shrinking body
Is a more peculiar way to die.

Yet in me is combat
Fought like this: the weird bat
Of soul, escapeless, will expire at

Length. Yet who will deny
A gaudy universe is nigh?
Not me. Yet who obstructs the seeing? I.

10 June [1940] TS

Poem

Still beauty,
o silent, happy
without change:
a blown bubble
a set tinge
no sun can rearrange –
can we, can
this not escape man?
this desperate desire
for relieved pain
of dissolution, for
no ash after fire!

No, a deathwish
only, you would cash.
a scudding ripple
of living, in the flesh
is only; a momentary apple,
a quick sundapple
frozen, are mute.
you also, my quick fruit
of bloom and sense,
eternity would defeat
although your decadence
indicts our scornful chance.

12 June [1940] TS, FP

[77]

'At once he realised that the thrilling night'

At once he realised that the thrilling night
Was changing into beauty, and that where
Had been a laughing and a grotesque sight
Stood now a scene of drama. Stars were near
And implicated: all the leaning trees
Shadowed their silent path with drifting air
Blown from the moon across the cloudy seas
Of sundown to him and his darling, there.

But life could not deceive him, for he knew
That moments such as these entailed a price
That he was marked to pay; and even though
It was so pleasant simply to agree,
He saw the present tense could not suffice
To pay these charges of futurity.

[*June 1940?*] TS (as 'Mary had a little lamb in Arabic') CHP (XVII;
as 'Two Versions (ii)'; (i) being 'Unexpectedly the scene attained')

Poem

Walking on summer grass beneath the trees
It is only the sprawling lovers that he sees,

And viewed from the embankment, autumn fires
Seem like symbols of many assuaged desires;

Schools interest him deeply, and members of teams,
Who possess what he avoids, except in dreams,

So receive his savage fits of gentleness
As befits one of his loneliness.

[1940?] TS

Prayer of a Plum

I am a ripe plum on a sunny wall;
Oh don't, don't shake me, or I'll fall.

For this great summer, as long as we remember,
Has burned right through, from April to September;

And now it's nearly done: yet still there wanders
Music at evening from the tall french windows,

When every dying rose attends, and we
Rest on the richest wall in history.

The violet sunset whispers: You have sinned.
But give us till we drop a gentle wind:

Although the anarchy of frost must come
Protect from Autumn gales each lucent plum:

And when the Winter fractures earth and sky
Let us have fallen, and in quietness lie.

[1940?] TS

'A bird sings at the garden's end'

A bird sings at the garden's end.

This evening all the backgardens are full of birds,
Past the road and the railway to the woods,
And the park, and the bridge at the river's bend,
Calling quietly in a cindered peace,
Where I and my shadow look each other in the face.

Shall I walk, with the mild sun touching
– in my shadow, running before me on the stone?
It hardens, and the clouds roll up for rain,
And I am unbrothered again, catching
At my pockets now the sun has gone –

No, it is back again; look at the sun.

This morning, with a swagger in my glance,
Money swording at my thigh, I strode
Casually up the forbidden road
To the station hiding in the trees and fence,
Bought a single ticket, saw a train,
Noted the black express was still dawn-due to run.

Shall I link hands with my shadow and stroll
Down the canal and over the railway bridge?
Recall the inn's stories: 'The city's rage
Will bite you, son, after the third stile.'
Shall I show myself a haunter of outgoing ways,
A longer, regretful at boundaries?

They are walking in pairs past the shut shops.

Through the streets, they and I pass,
And I see a devil shouting in their face,

But no word from either pair of lips
Mitigates the silence we employ . . .

A boy-linked shadow passes a girl and boy.

I run behind a tree and scribble notes:
  'The enemy fling into grass on sight;
  Play with cycles, get a pipe alight;
  Go shrieking out in foursomes in the boats;
  They wear greased foreheads. In the dark,
  Never leave the main paths in the park.'

I sit on the bank pulling out a letter
And the twelve white swans swim up for bread;
'Nothing for you,' I say, 'I'm going to read'
– Turn and catch a girl amazed in laughter
Ready to run and tell dad the very latest.

Shall I tell my shadow who I've missed?
Sit among the captains' tailored talk
Dark-sweatered, in the hotels [sic] mirrored bar,
Gaze like a wizard at my amber beer
That winks at me, and froths up when I walk?

Or leave my shadow in the yard
And sit behind french-windows with a word?

Shadow, run before me when we depart,
Run through the morning streets, sit on my side
Girder-flickered as we bridge the road
For the last time – how I taste that bit!
Oh, bold bad future, let me run away
And leave our quarrel till another day –
Yes, shadow, come and with me say goodbye
To the soldiers and the greengrocer's dog
And the bitch in the Woolpack that sold me a flag,

[82]

To the park, and the castle burnished on high,
The river and the racecourse and the canal
And the sandbags, falling down as usual;
From the train bursting into the sun
With the steam running rosy under the blue sky
I can throw my handfuls of bustickets away –

                        Shadow, when distance is done,
Leave us; when we meet
Be a lost shadow in the rest of the night.

(This MS has been badly gnawed by Flemish rabbits.)

[1940?] TS

Planes Passing

The guns
Tap the slack drumhead of the sky
Where separate bombers crawl,
Leaving soft trails of sound.
Time has run into the ground,
And the past squats upon the earth
Searching its fur for fleas.

Is life drinking, will it ever lift
Its head from drinking, and move
Delicately in an undreamt direction?
Or have these threads
Drawn and redrawn in the flesh of night
Sewn a dead parcel to be stuffed and stink
Under history's stairs?

The guns give an immediate answer.

[1940?] TS

[84]

'I should be glad to be in at the death'

I should be glad to be in at the death
Of our loud cities, wet hoardings,
Faces, and trivial assertive breath –
I should like to see the last of these things.

When I see the Sunday paper in the old-world cottage,
Main roads, or a fleet of delivery vans,
When I think how people have to earn a wage,
Then I want to lie down, and forget I'm a man,

Wishing the day would come, as it must,
When it will all go, all ploughed into line
With fields, and the plough itself stand to rust,
And nothing happen for a long time.

(from 'Poems for a National Day of Prayers', Faeber and
Fwaeber)

[1940?] TS

Chant

A trainload of tanks is leaving the town
A ship outside the harbour is going down
The sky's full of aeropanes [*sic*] overhead
And the streets are full of soldiers that are going to be dead.

Down to the factory go dad and mother
They go in one door, shells come out the other,
A letter told my sister she'd got to leave home
With a ticket for a very distant aerodrome.

Bought a paper printed on human skin
That told the living to keep smiling and the dead to grin,
Sat in the cinema and saw the News
Thought it was a horror film and looked down at my shoes.

Picked up a revolver and put it down again,
Travelled eighty miles in an express train,
Saw a poster staring with a picture of a bomb
Saw it was the station I'd started from.

Dreamed I was walking through a field of corn
And it was all men and women, chained where they were
    born,
The blades of the reaper turned in the sun
And nothing I could do would help anyone.

Went up on a mountain, looked as far as I could see,
The world was as dead as a petrified tree,
Only the sea moved up the shore
And all was winter for evermore.

[1940?] TS

'For who will deny'

For who will deny
A gaudy universe is nigh?
Not me. Yet who obstructs the seeing? I.

[*before July 1940*] FP (as epigraph)

After-Dinner Remarks

A good meal can somewhat repair
   The eatings of slight love;
And now the evening ambles near,
Softly, through the scented air,
Laying by the tautened fear:
   Peace sliding from above.

The trees stand in the setting sun,
   I in their freckled shade
Regard the cavalcade of sin,
Remorse for foolish action done,
That pass like ghosts regardless, in
   A human image made;

And as usual feel rather sad
   At the cathedral spire,
The calling birds that call the dead,
The waving grass that warns the glad,
I think of all that has been said
   About this faint desire;

Of where the other beings move
   Among this evening town,
Innocent of impendent grave,
Happy in their patterned groove,
Who do not need a light to save
   Or cheer when they lie down.

The handsome and the happy, cut
   In one piece from the rock;
With living flesh beneath their coat,

Who cannot their emotions glut,
And know not how to sneer or gloat.
    But only sing or mock,

To these my thoughts swing as a tide
    Turns to its sunny shore;
These I would choose my heart to lead
Instruct and clean, perhaps elide
What evil thought was bearing seed,
    And must spring up no more.

II

Pondering reflections as
    Complex and deep as these,
I saw my life as in a glass:
Set to music (negro jazz),
Coloured by culture and by gas,
    The idea of a kiss:

Contemptible: I quite agree,
    Now that the evening dies,
The sky proceeds from blue to grey
By imperceptible degree
And light and curtains drawn allay
    The vastness of the skies.

Stigmatised the exile who
    Cannot go from his land,
I in a dream of sea and hay,
Of kissing wind and merging blue
Think what I could have won today
    By stretching out my hand,

The challenge that I could proclaim
    The vows that I could swear;

Equipment to attempt the climb,
Or by straight love the world to tame,
What gesture in the face of time
  Could I have fashioned there.

Though living is a dreadful thing
  And a dreadful thing is it –
Life the niggard will not thank,
She will not teach who will not sing,
And what serves, on the final bank,
  Our logic and our wit?

III

Who for events to come to him
  May wait until his death:
Life will not violate his home
But leaves him to his evenings dim;
When all the world starts out to roam,
  She lets him save his breath.

What does he gain? Alas, relief
  Shrivels with his youth;
He will forget the way to laugh,
Cut off by his mental reef
From music hall and tall giraffe –
  He will distort the truth.

Against these facts this can be set –
  We do not make ourselves:
There is no point in such deceit,
To introspectively regret
Can never our defect defeat,
  Or mend our broken halves.

Those who are born to rot, delay –
　　And am I one of these?
A keyhole made without a key
A poem none can read or say,
A gate none open wide to see
　　The fountains and the trees.

Excuse for doing nothing, yes –
　　But I can still point out
That one can will and will for years
Be neither Aaron nor a Tess
But only see, through staling tears,
　　A quickly-spawning doubt.

IV

Choose what you can: I do remain
　　As neuter: and meanwhile
Exploding shrapnel bursts the men
Who thought perhaps they would disdain
The world that from its reechy den
　　Emerges with a smile;

All the familiar horrors we
　　Associate with others
Are coming fast along our way:
The wind is warning in our tree
And morning papers still betray
　　The shrieking of the mothers.

And so, while summer on this day
　　Enacts her dress rehearsals,
Let us forget who has to die,
Swim in the delicious bay,
Experience emotion by
　　The marvellous cathedrals;

Sad at our incompetence
   Yet powerless to resist
The eating bane of thought that weans
Us to a serious birthday whence
We realise the sterile 'teens
   And what we shall have missed

When all the lovely people that
   Instinct should have obeyed
Have passed us in our tub of thought,
As on this evening when we sat
Devoid of help from simple 'ought'
   Or resolution's aid.

Around, the night drops swiftly down
   Its veils; does not condemn
Or praise the different actions done.
The hour that strikes across the town
Caresses all and injures none
   As sleep approaches them.

[*before July 1940*] FP, CHP, CP

Two Sonnets

I: The conscript

So he evolved a saving fiction as
The moving world abraised him: in which he
Obeyed a self-writ charter: 'My soul is
A sacred centre, hid in folds; and who
Would violate its privacy would tear
The pleading rosebud to disclose its heart.'
And so he did not pray to his Creator,
Lounging aside, disdaining joy or hurt.

And when the world compelled him to killing
He heard no inner voices – none was calling,
There was no core of life within his bud
To animate his thoughts of good and bad,
And save his frozen heart, for all to see
Immobile in death's lovely tracery.

II: The conscientious objector

This was the first fruit of his new resolve –
The old loves sickened, and the starting point
Of one which might have proved as strong grown faint.
The stars that were so friendly now revolve
Without commenting on him; all that was neat,
Warm and familiar in the old regime
Pleads his return to their slick, ordered time,
And half of him obeys, welcomes defeat,

Disgrace. For that is all that it would be
Save safety – of a sort. If he persist
His northern way, love's lights and murmuring sea
Will drop behind; longer will grow the nights,

Shorter the days, till, lost amongst the mist,
He falls amid cold logic's stalactites.

[*before July 1940*] FP

Further afterdinner remarks (extempore)

I never was much of a one for beauty
  In leaf or life, not one to kindle
A chaste exquisiteness from duty –
  Always regard them somewhat as a swindle.

The moments living gives to stop our notions
  Like cook giving a plum to save the larder,
Or as a friendly capitalist gives good conditions
  To make his workers work so much the harder.

Keats and Shakespeare wrote a lot of verse –
  And very nice too, if you're bent that way –
But will it help when life grows quickly worse,
  Or will it answer when you question why?

This sun that's setting, how it gilds the houses!
  With bank on bank of arched clouds afire –
Now every trembling leaf speaks to me: 'Now is
  The time to kiss, to tremble, to expire! . . .'

This face I see before me – it is yours –
  Why must I penetrate its walls of flesh,
Why clairvoyantly see what the years
  Will do to make it just a wrinkled mesh

Tracing the bone? That has as little point
  As any trick you play of ecstasy,
Life, you stewed-up remainder of the joint:
  In such an argument we shan't agree

Not till the stars come down with the angels
  To greet me, and shake my hand in the public
Then I shall have a reason for changing square:
  My views, my life, my love, the style of my hair –

Perhaps, on that day, I shall be one for a spot
    Of beauty, in living and hoping, in mental prism
See reasons for everything about me, not
    A mere dweller on the other lip of the chasm

Watching the earth at play – I shall join them – the dresses!
    'Well played, sir!' from the side of the court at the fiery volley;
The beautiful symbolic hours as conversion progresses –
    'You're quite different from the rest' – 'Do you like Shelley?'

[*before July 1940*] FP

Ultimatum

But we must build our walls, for what we are
Necessitates it, and we must construct
The ship to navigate behind them, there.
Hopeless to ignore, helpless instruct
For any term of time beyond the years
That warn us of the need for emigration:
Exploded the ancient saying: Life is yours.

For on our island is no railway station,
There are no tickets for the Vale of Peace,
No docks where trading ships and seagulls pass.

Remember stories you read when a boy
– The shipwrecked sailor gaining safety by
His knife, treetrunk, and lianas – for now
You must escape, or perish saying no.

[*before July 1940*] *Listener*, 28 November 1940 FP, CP

Historical
Fact:

Shelley
had a belly.

[before July 1940] FP

Midsummer Night, 1940

The sun falls behind Wales; the towns and hills
Sculptured on England, wait again for night
As a deserted beach the tide that smoothes

Its rumpled surface flat: as pale as moths
Faces from factory pass home, for what respite
Home offers: crowds vacate the public halls:

And everywhere the stifling mass of night
Swamps the bright nervous day, and puts it out.
In other times, when heavy ploughmen snored,

And only some among the wealthy sneered,
On such a night as this twilight and doubt
Would mingle, and the night would not

Be day's exhaustion; there would drift about
Strange legends of the bridge across the weir,
Rings found in the grass, with undertone

Of darker terror, stories of the tarn,
The horned stranger, a pervading fear
No jolly laugh disperses. But

We, on this midsummer night, can sneer
In union at mind that could confuse
The moon and cheese, or trust in lightfoot images,

And point with conscious pride to our monstrosities
– Gained by no cerebral subterfuge,
Yet more convincing – a compulsory snare,

Expending of resources for the use
Of all the batty guardians of pain
– With no acknowledgement of pleasure, even –

The angels yawning in an empty heaven;
Alternate shows of dynamite and rain;
And choosing forced on free will: fire or ice.

June 1940 FP, CP

'But as to the real truth, who knows? The earth'

But as to the real truth, who knows? The earth
May yet bring forth, the past the future
Flowering over walls, a leaping urge –
And I, composer of life's dirge,
Be called upon to broadcast and to nurture:
Assist, not at a funeral, but a birth.

[*before July 1940*] FP

'It is late: the moon regards the city'

It is late: the moon regards the city,
Honeycombs of houses, each
Its nervous cell of light and pity.
Like the sun she cannot teach
The mad who with alacrity
Refuse to feel or comprehend;
Burn their nerves at either end,

Despite insane accoutrements,
Their colleges and churches, still
They cannot atrophy their sense
Entirely, and their maze of will
With all its taut accomplishments
Cannot prevent the sudden flashes
Of unrelated images

That print upon the brain as clear
As mountain's portraits in a lake;
Still for the North they blindly steer
But still their South's imploring ache
That cannot give or domineer
Offer it simple evidence
In unregarded incidents.

And the painter who can see
With an integrated eye
To make these separate shots agree
For every mind must try, must try:
Must in private purity
Teach all to see and to behave,
Loosing to hold; by losing, save.

August 1940 (for J. B. Sutton's birthday?, 23 August) TS

'A birthday, yes, a day without rain'

A birthday, yes, a day without rain
A cake but no candles, we're born again
The church cat is ordering cocktail glasses
The general's arranging the ensemble classes
The cissy is going for cross-country runs
We haven't much time, get ready at once:
For Jim
Goal-getter, holer-in-one,
Hurdler, high-jumper, hope of our side,
Our hush-hush engine, our wonder liner,
Our gadget, our pride,
Our steel-piercing bullet, our burglarproof safe
Will
Save . . .

August 1940 (letter to J. B. Sutton on his birthday, 23 August) TS

'Art is not clever'

Art is not clever
Art is not willing
Art is rather silly.

And for ever
Art has been recalcitrant
To the searcher who has meant
To capture art and glory like a swan.

Art is the performing
Of the single act
Of love or accepted duty:
Is sometimes beauty,
But is always the statement
Of the simple fact.

[*before September 1940*] PAug40, CHP

'Unexpectedly the scene attained'

Unexpectedly the scene attained
Traditional aptness. Everything was there:
The stars; the darling; and the pathway, veined
By moonlight through the trees; the drifting air
That, quickened by the waters' imminence,
Cooled the hot palm and stirred the sticky hair.
All assumed its rightful prominence
To strike the pose.
                    Time rearranged the pair;
And yet there came from life no counterthrust,
No gentle summer sky was overcast,
No recompense demanded – only trust,
So that she could prepare her blow to shatter,
Her lianas grow to stifle; as in the past
With others, whose names now no longer matter.

[*before September 1940*] PAug40, CHP (xvii; as 'Two Versions (i)',
(ii) being 'At once he realised that the thrilling night')

Address to Life, by a Young Man Seeking a Career

Freckling summers have crossed my brow
    To the number of just eighteen;
And I know that I should be deciding now
    To what profession I lean;
All others with whom I have spent my youth
    Have chosen their own avenue,
Yet (though I'm ashamed to tell you the truth)
    There's nothing that *I* want to do.

Life, you are busy, I appreciate that,
    Arranging for everyone;
But I really think we should have a chat
    About what I am going to become;
I've really tried to discover your aims
    Whatever their nature and kind,
But, although not the sort of a fellow who blames
    – I think I've slipped out of your mind.

Do you want me to work and to gain a degree
    And to live in the shade of the spires?
Do you want me to study philosophy
    Or catalogue human desires?
Do you want me to be the authority
    On Milton and Dryden and Pope?
If this is the future you've mapped out for me,
    Then why don't you give me some hope?

(You don't, I suppose, really propose
    To make me a student of science:
If that is your wish, I'm afraid I oppose
    With a gently stubborn defiance;
For everyone knows that I fall in a doze
    When faced with a real microscope;

And if you chose this, the facts interpose,
  And thus there is really no hope.)

And Classics as well can all go to hell
  For I've acted upon your advice;
I've again and again thrown them all down the drain
  For I never supposed they were nice.
Thus it is clear that a scholar's career
  Doesn't seem to be your little plan;
But why won't you speak? For every week
  Is pushing me nearer the Pan.

Or do you intend I should regally spend
  A fortune, and live like a king?
To live between Greece and Paris and Nice?
  I don't think I should like such a thing:
– And first you must give the means thus to live,
  Before I can safely smirk;
For at present you see it does look to me
  As if I shall have to work.

Life, what is your aim? I say it again:
  Direct and control my inquiries;
I've poured out my woes in poems and prose
  And even in several diaries;
See, I invite you to teach me to write
  On my psychological squalls;
You will not comply, and, although I do try,
  The result is invariably · · · · ·.

Therefore I am not a don or a swot
  Or a dandy who grinds down the poor;
I'm not such a blighter to think I'm a writer
  When others so obviously are.
Do you think, perhaps, I'm one of the chaps
  Who is either a Bull or a Bear?

Although it is funny, when it comes to money
　　I'm really no earthly good there.

Although not an Eric, shall I be a cleric
　　And sermonise every Sunday?
That would be a trick that would make me quite sick
　　From Saturday right through to Monday;
I've tried being good, and I don't think I could,
　　And I never get very excited,
So I let fall a tear for the Bishop's career
　　To which I was never invited.

And similarly, I shan't be an M.P.
　　Although I could burble quite well;
If you think of the Army – well, Life, you're just barmy,
　　– Though of course one can never quite tell –
I belong to no faction of people of action
　　Whether pacifist, fascist or red,
In actual fact, I never could act,
　　Because I am more than half dead.

This long catalogue is a wearisome job
　　And it's one that you, Life, ought to do:
My predestined fate I quietly await,
　　The choosing is all up to you.
Whatever proposal, if at my disposal,
　　I'll follow with loyalty blind;
But the earth's getting colder, and I'm growing older –
　　So please won't you make up your mind?

　　　　　[before September 1940] PAug40

　　　　　[MS] Postscript 1943

　　I'm sorry to say that, as life looks today,
　　　　I'm going to reside out in Wellington,

Where everyone's rude, and ashamed of a nude,
    And nobody's heard of Duke Ellington;
Life, you aren't a god, you're a bloody old sod
    For giving me such an employment
'Cos in such a bad job only pulling my knob
    Will bring me the slightest enjoyment.

29 November 1943

How true, how true, how true

10 August 1944

'O today is everywhere'

O today is everywhere
Summer's warm sincerity
And her landscapes all appear
Ranged in easy poetry;
Shadows dark against the hedges
On the further side of fences;
Hot all sloping sides of roofs
And small unconsidered ledges
Near the sky, where sparrows roost.
Flies are buzzing in the privet,
Bees are dropping to their coloured
Landing grounds of green and gold.
Now there can be nothing private
The endless roads lead everywhere
The skimming wind caresses all
The sun's including stare is equal:
Everything upon this island
Runs from valley up to tor
Drops from cavern down to plain
In a sweep of harvest corn
Ending at the farmer's home,
Or among the rocks, alone,
In the sea's rejoicing spume.

[*before September 1940*] PAug40

[110]

'There are moments like music, minutes'

There are moments like music, minutes
Untroubled as notes that hang
Motionless, invisible on air:
Here the individual is eased from his fear,
His knotted life, and everything in it:
For here is no logic or harangue,

Here is the simple, pointless existence of art,
Fact as plain as a child's demand: why
Is the sun red? Here are hours
Only shown by moving shadows of flowers,
Long as poised beats of heart,
Drifting like waters of eternity,

And with dignity like chords of an organ
Descending in great flights of stone,
Solid, for ever here. Nothing to do
But look. Day opens into day.
And, certain of ultimate hearing, even the known
Problems may briefly turn their gaze from man.

[*before September 1940*] PAug40, CHP

Creative Joy

Anything or nothing
Can release his writing
The dream recollection
Of face or anything
From beauty to decay
Compels instant attention
At that hour of that day:
Demands immediate attempt
And his full strength.

An hour past, a page
Threequarters done
The demand of the sun
Draws him from doors
Returning to rows
Scolding in defeated rage.

[*before September 1940*] PAug40

'As a war in years of peace'

As a war in years of peace
Or in war an armistice
Or a father's death, just so
Our parting was not visualized
When from the further side I gazed
Occasionally, as likely sorrow,

For parting is no single act
Scenery-shifting for the next,
Parting is a trailing streamer,
Lingering like leaves in autumn
Thinning at the winter's comb –
No more impressive nor supremer;

If so, then still is less than death,
The only parting; on a hearth
Or passing street, always the meeting
And the wondering brain and eye
Quickly consulting memory
To follow or precede the greeting.

Only another case, perhaps,
Arranges our predestined shapes:
That of brilliant passing liner,
Or the miraculous interpretation
Of the simple composition –
Jewels life throws up like a miner.

And so, being caught quite unawares
By petition for some gracious tears,
I ponder on the consequence
Of never seeing this, nor saying
What, remembered, still seems glowing
As all of you. Indifference?

[Revised Version: September 1942]

As a war in years of peace
Or in war an armistice
Or a father's death, just so
I could not visualise us parted:
From the other side regarded
It did not seem a likely sorrow.

But parting is no simple act
Making way for what comes next:
Parting is a trailing streamer
Lingering like leaves in autumn
Thinning at the winter's comb –
Fading like a marching drummer.

And the throbbing disappears
And I have no gracious tears
To ponder on the consequence
Of having seen you drown and die
In my personal history:
And can this be indifference?

Note by Larkin: 'Written August 1940: revised September
15th 1942. Coventry-Warwick. This is the first instance of a
poem being revised.' PAug40, CHP, CP

'Could wish to lose hands'

Could wish to lose hands
And feet, their touching and their being,
    Obstinate with their nails
    Neat termination. And

Pointing them like conductors of lightning
At clouds, call down energy and fire
    Inwards; or perhaps as
    A dying man lose knowledge

Of them and their doing; or as the Nile,
Splayed in a delta as these fingers are,
    Pours out its individual stream
    Diffusedly, and is lost in the sea.

[*before September 1940*] PAug40, CHP

'The spaniel on the tennis court'

The spaniel on the tennis court
Nuzzles his shadow as he runs,
Oblivious of a cooling earth
And various human skeletons;

He does not try to seem sincere
Sincerity is not his job;
Nor beauty, either of himself
Or any other of the mob.

His scraps appear like striking hours;
Doors wait ajar for him at night;
The hands that move above his head
Do not affect his appetite.

He's happy? Good. He's ill? If that,
Unhappy snivels in the warm:
He's confident? Chases a 'bus:
Afraid? There is a thunderstorm.

Nothing is his. The tennis court
To him is Paradise; with reason:
He has a great advantage for
There is no serpent in his Eden.

[*before September 1940*] PAug40

Schoolmaster

He sighed with relief. He had got the job. He was safe.
Putting on his gown, he prepared for the long years to
    come
That he saw, stretching like aisles of stone
Before him. He prepared for the unreal life
Of exercises, marks, honour, speech days and games,
And the interesting and pretty animals that inspired it all,
And made him a god. No, he would never fail.

Others, of course, had often spoken of the claims
Of living: they were merely desperate.
His defence of Youth and Service silenced it.

It was acted as he planned: grown old and favourite,
With most Old Boys he was quite intimate –
For though he never realised it, he
Dissolved. (Like sugar in a cup of tea.)

    [*before September 1940*] PAug40, CHP, CP

'When we broke up, I walked alone'

When we broke up, I walked alone
   And walked into the Hall;
And saw long sheets of manuscript
   All nailed up on the wall;

I pulled them down, quite thinking
   That they were by some japer,
For they were written in capitals
   Upon some lavatory paper;

However, I don't think this was so
   – Although it may have been –
But I will print them here for you,
   And you can learn their theme:

'When I was eight, I came to school
   With large and curious eyes,
Imagining that everyone
   Was of enormous size;

'Yes, I was eight years old when I
   Toddled in with Doubt;
And Doubt is still my fellow as
   Eighteen, I saunter out.

'O, I am educated
   For I have been told so –
You'd really be surprised, my dear,
   At all the things I know.

'When I was twelve years old, I learnt
   How to add a to b,
And how the Romans said "I love"
   And when the French say "thee".

'And I learnt how the tundra
   Behaves up in the North,
And all about the prairies,
   And ships in the Firth of Forth.

'And I was taught how Jesus
   Had come to save my soul,
And all about the Pyramids,
   And how to play in goal.

'When I was a sweet fifteen
   I learnt about the dead,
I learnt how when an acid's near
   A litmus paper's red.

'I learnt about the triangles
   And their peculiar ways,
I learnt some poetry about
   "Lime-blossoms in a haze".

'When I was a sweet sixteen
   I began to specialise:
I learnt to read the poets
   And to write a lot of lies.

'And also read some Molière,
   And a little Hugo too,
And learnt what Garibaldi said
   In 1862.

'And I can give statistics
   About Roumania's oil,
And talk about the country
   (Productivity of soil)

'And I have read the poets
   Yes, every bloody one:
From Langland up to Shelley
   And from Auden back to Donne.

'And O my hair is wavy
   And O my eyes are soft
And O my smile is gentle
   And my thoughts are up aloft:

'O yes my hair is wavy
   But it comes out by the roots,
And falls in golden strands about
   My neatly-polished boots.

'O yes my eyes are gentle;
   And yet my mind is quicker,
For I read eleven hours a day
   And my specs are getting thicker.

'And though my smile is kindly
   My teeth are rotting in my head,
And though my thoughts are up aloft
   My lower half is dead.

'O what am I becoming
   Who is so brilliant?
Shall I become quite famous?
   Sometimes I think I shan't.

'Sometimes I think that you, sir,
   Have killed your lovely duck,
And I shall lay no golden eggs
   For you to gloat and cluck;

'I think your education
    Has maimed my better half
And has blown up my other side
    With cubic feet of gas.

'O I wish I wish I wish I were
    Anyone but myself:
For though my mind is in the skies
    My body's on the shelf.

'And there are awful crimes I know
    And men who don't succeed,
But they are at least more interesting
    Than what I can achieve.

'O teach me how to live a life
    And be as all men should,
O teach me what is earth, and fire,
    And what resides in wood.

'O teach me to recognise the false
    And recreate the true:
Make me forget the verb "to know"
    Remember "be" and "do".

'O teach me why the stars, and birds,
    And I myself are one:
For I your victim ask that you
    Undo the harm you've done.'

[*before September 1940*] PAug40

'From the window at sundown'

From the window at sundown
Walking out onto grass
I receive intimation
Of the usual peace.

Harvests lie
Resting in sheaves across
The arching fields.
Sounds fall on moss;

Are deadened; die.
The village is there
As for years;
Its bells shake gently the air

I breathe; breathing
Try imagining contrast
Between this peace
And my veiled holocaust.

But emotion under
Guise of reason says:
You are the motivator; no,
You are this peace.

[*before September 1940*] PAug40, CHP

'You've only one life and you'd better not lose it'

'You've only one life and you'd better not lose it,
No good protesting that you didn't choose it;
Whoever's responsible, you'll have to pay,
And you're only alive for a Year and a Day.

'Your spring is so lovely, you don't realise:
You gaze at the world with great big eyes;
These are the days when you will, as a rule,
Feel like a genius and think like a fool.

'Then comes the summer: you think you're mature,
And possibly marry, you're so very sure;
Or perhaps you scorn others, and travel among
The sweeping giraffes, in the lands of the sun.

'Autumn perhaps is the greatest of fun:
You lose your belief in the things that you've done;
The bank clerk reflects that his pay isn't large:
The professor's had up on a serious charge.

'Winter creeps out of his legendary lair,
But it isn't so bad, 'cos you're only half there,
Just a failing machine that awaits termination,
A pest to yourself and your nearest relation.

'That is your Year; on the Day you deny
Your whole way of life; see The Truth; and then die;
You cannot convey and there's noone to hear
So you give up the struggle and just disappear.

'Yes, living is hard, but there were others before;
So sit on your hands and hold your jaw;
Make a fool of yourself, for nobody minds;
And soon enough for you they'll pull down the blinds.'

Envoi

Darling, I wrote the preceeding review
When you'd done something I hoped you'd do;
So doesn't it shake your simple faith
In the Perfectibility of the Human Race?

[*before September 1940*] PAug40

'The question of poetry, of course'

The question of poetry, of course,
Is difficult: some say a poet should
Mix with his fellows, be a social force;
Others say he should be simply good;
Others, that he should be a Communist;
Perhaps a scholar, even drive a van;
Or spend his waking hours in being kissed;
Or all these, and become a Complete Man.

Myself, I think that poetry is merely
The Ego's protest at the world's contempt,
And that there are no normal poets, really.
Therefore, if as tonight, dear, he should move
In motions of spending and the acts of love,
He has lived his poem; all his power is spent.

[*before September 1940*] PAug40

Rupert Brooke

Give him his due – some liked his poetry;
And certainly he had an influence
While living as a man; his eloquence
Can move; and with friends life passed happily
With opening spring-time in a Warwick garden,
Alone in Munich, or in warm Tahiti
Before exploding war returned him quickly
To write five sonnets that the old have taken.

Indeed, he was perfect like an apple – but there were
Hints of an unsound core: opthalmic at Rugby,
Nervous at Cambridge, rarely in good health;
Poisoned by coral and water; sun's enemy;
Brothers and friends all dead, some killed in the war –
Yes, his blood wrote poems; both foretold his death.

[*before September 1940*] PAug40

Postscript
On Imitating Auden

Imitating you is fairly easy
Because you have but one sincerity,
Whereas most people – I as well – have two:
One to themselves, one to the good and true.
As in you they are synonymous
My allegiance to the good is obvious
To lead me to you. Perhaps is beneficial
To adopt the breezy tone, in general,
Of one who's Pure-in-Heart, but there is danger.
One's character betrayed may turn to anger,
And fill its tortuous streets with revolution,
Making the resonant hollow, the laughing
Greasy. May have happened. The solution
I do not know, but have been wondering
That when walking on your by-pass road,
Straight and clean and windy, shall be amazed
To reach the Other Town of light and action,
Far from all reticence and putrefaction,
And be compelled to face the expectant look
Of thousands, without money, home, or book.

[*before September 1940*] PAug40

'There is no language of destruction for'

There is no language of destruction for
The use of the chaotic; silence the only
Path for those hysterical and lonely.
That upright beauty cannot banish fear,
Or wishing help the weak to gain the fair
Is reason for it: that the skilled event,
Gaining applause, cannot a death prevent,
Short-circuits impotent who travel far.

And no word can be spoken of which the sense
Does not accuse and contradict at once.
And he gets no assistance from the world
Which will not help his looking into words,
Nor will the lovely, gay as any leaf,
Assuage his anguish. And the lions laugh.

1940 CHP, CP

Last Will and Testament
(with Noel Hughes)

Anxious to publicise and pay our dues
Contracted here, we, Bernard Noel Hughes
And Philip Arthur Larkin, do desire

To requite and to reward those whom we choose;
To thank our friends, before our time expire,
And those whom, if not friends, we yet admire.

First, our corporeal remains we give
Unto the Science Sixth – demonstrative
Of physical fitness – for minute dissection;

Trusting that they will generously forgive
Any trifling lapses from perfection,
And give our viscera their close attention.

– With one exception: we bequeath our ears
To the Musical Society, and hope
It finds out why they loathed the panatrope –

(And, however pointed it appears,
We leave the wash-bowls twenty cakes of soap)
Item, herewith to future pioneers

In realms of knowledge, we bequeath our books,
And woe pursue who to a master quotes
The funnier of our witty marginal notes.

Likewise, we leave the Modern Sixth the jokes
This year has fostered, and to him who croaks
Of Higher School Certificates, ten sore throats.

Item, our school reports we leave the Staff,
To give them, as we hope, a hearty laugh;
And Kipling's 'If' to hang upon their wall.

Sympathy for the impossible task
Of teaching us to swim the six-beat crawl
We leave our swimming master. Item, all

Our *Magnets* and our *Wizards* we consign
To the Librarian in the cause of Culture
And may his Library flourish well in future;

Next (now the troops have taken their departure)
With ever-grateful hearts we do assign
To our French master, all the Maginot Line.

Essays, and our notes on style and diction,
We leave our English master, confident
He won't consider them as an infliction.

Our German master, for the sore affliction
Of teaching us, we humbly present
With an Iron Cross (First Class, but slightly bent);

To the Art Master, as the only one
Appreciative (and, Philistines to thwart)
We leave a blue cap and four ties that stun:

And all the Scholarships we never won
We give to those who want things of that sort:
And to the Savings Groups . . . our full support.

Our Games Master we leave some high-jump stands
– The reason why we know he understands –
And to the Carpenter the grass he's mown.

To Paul Montgomery, a sturdy comb
To discipline his rough and ruddy strands;
And Mr H.B. Gould we leave . . . alone.

We leave our Latin cribs to William Rider,
And may his shadow never disappear;
To the Zoologists, a common spider;

And, for their services throughout the year,
To the Air Defence Cadets a model glider;
And to the First XV a cask of beer.

Item, to Percy Slater we now send
A candle he can burn at either end,
And hours of toil without the ill-effects;

Our badges we resign to future Prefects,
The lines-book, too; to F.G. Smith, our friend,
We leave a compact and a bottle of Cutex;

And all the paper that we never needed
For this *Coventrian*, to Ian Fraser,
And may he triumph where we've not succeeded:

To his subordinates, an ink eraser . . .
And this Magazine itself? Well, there's always a
Lot of people queer enough to read it.

Herewith we close, with Time's apology
For the ephemeral injury,
On this 26th of July, 1940.

The Coventrian, September 1940 CP

'The earliest machine was simple'

The earliest machine was simple:
Could clock the blue revolving days,
    Their single rain and sun
That fell uncensored to their grass;
Easy then with facile grace
    An unintentional symbol
That quickly and unnoticed dies,
    Its power done,

Gone from those fields; to where desires
Like icefloes breaking in the Spring
    Their crude procession make;
Earnest and, yes, dangerous days
Garish with exciting dyes
    In terms of blood and fires,
And love, that trap of logic, sprung
    By silent lake.

But the endless tidal splinter
That the sway of blood contains
    Those desires destroys,
Destroys their images of life,
While the fine selfconscious laugh
    Is shrivelled to a whimper
In uncertain, plaintive tones
    Of pervert's joys.

Yes, joy is a long way from here,
And the distance far enough
    To veil the primal curse
That planned, will plan, is planning now
For us, and those we shall not know,
    This course that, year by year,

Leading from fire to ash will leave
A Christian; or worse.

[*Autumn 1940*] TS

'At the flicker of a letter'

At the flicker of a letter
Brought from smashed city under frozen sky
In late November, at the year's sombre ending –
I at a tall window standing
Watch the tumultuous clouds go by,
Go by over field and street, college and river.

What they must not say
At this letter is awaking,
Is skimming like leaves that scatter,
As these few leaves that loiter
On the wet bough shaking –
Is awake, and can a hearing justify:

'Admit your detection, ostentatiously understanding,
But sad in a corner at arrival of your letter;
Confess that no man can deny
His ultimate reliance on his silly way;
May seek another but shall find no better,
No better to love, and none so unending.'

November 1940 7COL (year given by Larkin in preface; a slightly
different version of the first stanza is quoted in a letter to J. B.
Sutton, 20 December 1940)

Christmas 1940

'High on arched fields I stand
Alone: the night is full of stars:
Enormous over tree and farm
   The night extends,
And looks down equally on all earth.

'So I return their look; and laugh
To see them as my living stars
Flung from east to west across
   A windless gulf!
– So much to say that I have never said,
   Or ever could.'

20 December 1940 (letter to J. B. Sutton) MS, SL

Ghosts

They said this corner of the park was haunted,
At tea today, laughing through windows at
The frozen landscape. One of them recounted
The local tale: easy where he sat
With lifted cup, rocked in the servile flow
Of disbelief around, to understand
And bruise. But something touched a few
Like a slim wind with an accusing hand –
Cold as this tree I touch. They knew, as I,
Those living ghosts who cannot leave their dreams,
And in years after and before their death
Return as they can, and with ghost's pleasure search
Those several happy acres, or those rooms
Where, like unwilling moths, they collided with
The enormous flame that blinded and hurt too much.

21 December 1940 (letter to J. B. Sutton) MS, SL

'Out in the lane I pause: the night'

Out in the lane I pause: the night
Impenetrable round me stands,
And overhead, where roofline ends,
    The starless sky
Black as a bridge: the only light
Gleams from the little railway
    That runs nearby.

From the steep road that travels down
Towards the shops, I hear the feet
Of lonely walkers in the night
    Or lingering pairs;
Girls and their soldiers from the town
Who in the shape of future years
    Have equal shares;

But not tonight are questions posed
By them; no, nor the bleak escape
Through doubt from endless love and hope
    To hate and terror;
Each in their double Eden closed
They fail to see the gardener there
    Has planted Error;

Nor can their wish for quiet days
Be granted; though their motions kiss
This evening, and make happiness
    Plain as a book,
They must pursue their separate ways
And flushed with puzzled tears, turn back
    Their puzzled look.

And if, as of gipsy at a fair,
 Sorry, I inquire for them

If things are really what they seem,
    The open sky
And all the gasping, withered air
Can only answer: 'It is so'
    In brief reply.

So through the dark I walk, and feel
The ending year about me lapse,
Dying, into its formal shapes
    Of field and tree;
And think I hear its faint appeal
Addressed to all who seek for joy,
    But mainly me:

'From those constellations turn
Your eyes, and sleep; for every man
Is living; and for peace upon
    His life should rest;
This must everybody learn
For mutual happiness; that trust
    Alone is best.'

Christmas 1940 CHP, CP

New Year Poem

The short afternoon ends, and the year is over;
Above trees at the end of the garden the sky is unchanged,
An endless sky; and the wet streets, as ever,
Between standing houses are empty and unchallenged.
From roads where men go home I walk apart
– The buses bearing their loads away from works,
Through the dusk the bicycles coming home from bricks –
There evening like a derelict lorry is alone and mute.

These houses are deserted, felt over smashed windows,
No milk on the step, a note pinned to the door
Telling of departure: only shadows
Move when in the day the sun is seen for an hour,
Yet to me this decaying landscape has its uses:
To make me remember, who am always inclined to forget,
That there is always a changing at the root,
And a real world in which time really passes.

For even together, outside this shattered city
And its obvious message, if we had lived in that peace
Where the enormous years pass over lightly
– Yes, even there, if I looked into your face
Expecting a word or a laugh on the old conditions,
It would not be a friend who met my eye,
Only a stranger would smile and turn away,
Not one of the two who first performed these actions.

For sometimes it is shown to me in dreams
The Eden that all wish to recreate
Out of their living, from their favourite times;
The miraculous play where all their dead take part,
Once more articulate; or the distant ones
They will never forget because of an autumn talk

By a railway, an occasional glimpse in a public park,
Any memory for the most part depending on chance.

And seeing this through that I know that to be wrong,
Knowing by the flower the root that seemed so harmless
Dangerous; and all must take their warning
From these brief dreams of unsuccessful charms,
Their aloof visions of delight, where Desire
And Fear work hand-in-glove like medicals
To produce the same results. The bells
That we used to await will not be rung this year,

So it is better to sleep and leave the bottle unopened;
Tomorrow in the offices the year on the stamps will be altered;
Tomorrow new diaries consulted, new calendars stand;
With such small adjustments life will again move forward
Implicating us all; and the voice of the living be heard:
'It is to us that you should turn your straying attention;
Us who need you, and are affected by your fortune;
Us you should love and to whom you should give your word.'

31 *December* 1940 CHP, CP

Story

Tired of a landscape known too well when young:
The deliberate shallow hills, the boring birds
Flying past rocks; tired of remembering
The village children and their naughty words,
He abandoned his small holding and went South,
Recognised at once his wished-for lie
In the inhabitants' attractive mouth,
The church beside the marsh, the hot blue sky.

Settled. And in this mirage lived his dreams,
The friendly bully, saint, or lovely chum
According to his moods. Yet he at times
Would think about his village, and would wonder
If the children and the rocks were still the same.

But he forgot all this as he grew older.

Cherwell, 13 February 1941, CHP, CP

'The house on the edge of the serious wood'

The house on the edge of the serious wood
      Was aware, was aware
      Of why he came there,
And the reticent toad never told what it knew
When from the wet bracken it saw him pass through;
And round the next corner a tree poked its head:
'He's coming; be careful; pretend to be dead.'

Down on the river the swans sailed on,
      And on flowed the river
      For ever and ever
Over the interlocked counties and shires,
But never revealed that they knew his desires;
Reflected him walking alone in the sun,
And smiled at each other when he had gone.

On the school field at the edge of the town
      Where surely the secret
      Would not be so sacred
And might any moment materialise
He looked at the juniors with hopeful eyes
– But none of them moved until he had gone,
Then the game went on, the game went on.

No, neither the wood nor river nor child
      Showed as they should
      The True and the Good
Like a valley in blossom or plain as snow,
For they rather resented what he wished them to do;
Imagined he wished them to mirror his mind
That grew like a sapling and orchid combined;

But for once they were wrong: for the motives of acts
      Are rarely the same

As their name, as their name;
And they were not aware of his previous tours
Upon southern Alps, across northern moors,
Seeking in one place always another,
And travelling further from mother, from mother:

No, they were not told of the willing lanes,
        The black mill-pond
        Of which he was fond;
The warm and the narrow, the shadowed, the queer
As opposed to the open, the broad and the clear,
These strange dark patterns of his heart's designs
That would only respond to secret signs

That signalled in attics and gardens like Hope,
        And ever would pass
        From address to address,
As he watched from windows in the failing light
For his world that was always just out of sight
Where weakness was part of the ordinary landscape
And the friendly road knew his footstep, his footstep.

  before April 1941 CHP, CP

'Time and Space were only their disguises'

Time and Space were only their disguises
Under which their hatred chose its shapes
From swords in bushes, flowers like periscopes,
And mirrors that revealed themselves as faces.

And later, clouds flew past me as I sat;
Stations like ships swam up to meet the train
And bowed; all time was equal like the sun;
Each landscape was elaborately set.

But now this blackened city in the snow
Argues a will that cannot be my own,
And one not wished for: points to show

Time in his little cinema of the heart
Giving a première to Hate and Pain;
And Space urbanely keeping us apart.

before April 1941 CHP, CP

[144]

'Evening, and I, young'

Evening, and I, young,
Watch the single star beyond
The quiet road and trees;
Move in time and know
The evenings of the tired who died
Under their guardian hill:
Move in space and realise
The ones I love in lighted rooms
Their movements and their peace.

But who can tell the many myriad stars?
Not I, not I, though soon I must face them and feel
The light night wind singing against my eyes.
Stand on a hill, or lean from dark window –
The stars in their intricate patterns will daze
Any who stare; useless to try to order their mass,
Their number, they are balanced in system
Which you cannot better. What was simple
And moving, a note on a single string,
Now it flings jagged colours, rehearses
Orchestras of sound and rhythm to your dazzled ears,
Eyes, nor can see, grasp with mazed mind.
If you must, as I must, gaze at their whirling
Miraculous display, nothing can save
From the cascading mind, the rocks that receive
The final crashing turrets of the brain.

From this chaos, what result? Watch:
Night wears through its hours at last, and
Again we stand where we stood, watching a single star
By the stark tree on the hill, and think
Of faces, webbed with decay, that once
Pulled us protesting through sunlight on water,
Rain on grass: the rusted hands rest on a stick.

O love then, for there is little time for them,
For then east sky is white and the star will fade,
The last stronghold will fall, day pass, defence vanish,
And we depart as we came, with a pale star,
Shading our eyes before death's imminent sun.

[*before April 1941*] CHP

'Stranger, do not linger'

Stranger, do not linger
Though you feel stronger
Their darling languor;
Balloons in evening swaying
Cast on this meadow
Their moving shadow,
And tall grass saying
'Always remain', may seem
Happy to some,
Happy and unafraid.
Be not deceived
Believing them saved;
Only their weakness calls,
Captures, and then kills
Who wrong choice has made;
With unconscious terror
Has run to hide in mirror;
Now, trusting no singer,
Commits the fatal error,
Can sight no anger
Can sate no hunger.

[*before April 1941*] CHP

'Out of this came danger'

Out of this came danger
    And sudden anger
For grace is stronger
    Than any singer
And every place
    Reveals its face
Till sunlit grass
    Shall flower and pass.
In ancient years
    Where childhood's tears
Like mended tears
    Prevent the seers
A falling rock
    A fading rick
Across the rake
    Where cattle reek
These too will show
    Where sinks the snow
And on their shore
    Where love is shy
But till this come
    As others came
The mental comb
    Shall irk and scream
Shall in its place
    Shatter the splice
Attack the grace
    Wither grass
    In paradise.

[*before April 1941*] (from a 6-part poem, only two and a bit parts existing. This is part (v): (vi) is 'Several eagles crossed my page' in CHP) TS

The Poet's Last Poem

Several eagles crossed my page
I put down my pen
Returning from a pilgrimage
So many separate men
Lifted their hands in the air
Pointed at heaven
Sun flashed on rings there
Seven times seven.
'Pass by,' I told them
'Reckers of rocks,
Here is no golden,
Dreamed-of box.'

Ponds of agate and crystal,
Apples of rubies,
Diamonded inkwells,
Wait for my hand;
Desmond in diamonds
Lawrence in laurels
David in garnets
Wait for me there, là-bas, there . . .

[*before April 1941*] TS, CHP

'The world in its flowing is various; as tides'

The world in its flowing is various; as tides,
Or stars arrayed, has rules imposed
By others on it as their personal guides.
To dig, divert, mark out, and to enclose
The plot of life bequeathed to each, or
File and order all diverse reports
Sent in from outposts of the hand and ear
– Simple their language that the brain distorts –
That is the mind's natural destructiveness
Aiding its plea for reason; even so
Its charts and plans are made in readiness.

And yet, as tides in winter when
The glass is sunk, incalculable flow
Of life can break down mortared walls, drown men.

[*before April 1941*] CHP (as (i) of 'Two Preliminary Sonnets';
(ii) is 'But we must build our walls, for what we are')

A Writer

'Interesting, but futile,' said his diary,
Where day by day his movements were recorded
And nothing but his loves received inquiry;
He knew, of course, no actions were rewarded,
There were no prizes: though the eye could see
Wide beauty in a motion or a pause,
It need expect no lasting salary
Beyond the bowels' momentary applause.

He lived for years and never was surprised:
A member of his foolish, lying race
Explained away their vices: realised
It was a gift that he possessed alone:
To look the world directly in the face;
The face he did not see to be his own.

Cherwell, 8 May 1941 CHP, CP

'At school, the acquaintance'

At school, the acquaintance
May come from daily glance
Or willing circumstance;

Or later, a letter
Reveals a mild hater
And wish to know better.

The occasional meeting
Shows time deflating
The need of mating;

Shows stronger need,
A narrower greed,
But be afraid

Of closer look,
To smiling speak
Of leaf and rock;

For this is likeness
Not of greatness
But weakness and weakness.

21 May 1941 (letter to J. B. Sutton) MS

May Weather

[VERSION 1]

A month ago in fields
Rehearsals were begun;
The stage that summer builds
And confidently holds
Was floodlit by the sun
And habited by men.

But parts were not correct:
The gestures of the crowd
Invented to attract
Need practice to perfect,
And balancing of cloud
With sunlight must be made;

So awkward was this May
Then training to prepare
Summer's impressive lie –
Upon whose every day
So many ruined are
May could not make aware.

Cherwell, 5 June 1941 TS, CP

[VERSION 2]

A week ago today
Rehearsals were begun,
The stage that summer builds
And confidently holds
Was floodlit by the sun
And habited by men.

But parts were not correct;
The gestures of the crowd
Invented to attract
Need practice to perfect
And balancing of cloud
With sunlight must be made;

So awkward is this May,
Now training to prepare
Summer's enormous lie,
Upon whose every day
So many ruined are
May could not make aware.

before February 1942 (but later than
Cherwell pub.) TS, 7P

'The wind at creep of dawn'

The wind at creep of dawn
Through arches and spires
Swells, and on the lawn
Manoeuvres, alone;

Who kept planes like desires
Back in alien shires
Last night, this daybreak pass
Where misery has signed

Every unhappy face,
And, wind, in meetingplace
Of wish and fear, be kind
In dreams to each unconsummated mind.

before 15 June 1941 (quoted in letter to J. B. Sutton) 7COL
(year given by Larkin in Preface)

[155]

'There behind the intricate carving'

There behind the intricate carving
A great conqueror is living,
Who in choice of book can prove
Scholarship's impersonal love,
Can in touch of hand imply
The sport's familiarity,
In movement of an eyebrow show
That all can pardon when all know.

Yet certain cruder literature
Or illegible signature
Or a voice singing, can arouse
A spirit from its ancient house,
Can send him wishing on a journey
Camouflaged among the many
Whose tangible and mountain ranges
Hide his microscopic changes.

[*before June 15 1941*] (quoted in letter to
J. B. Sutton, 15 June 1941) 7P

Conscript

for James Ballard Sutton

The ego's county he inherited
From those who tended it like farmers; had
All knowledge that the study merited,
The requisite contempt of good and bad;

But one Spring day his land was violated;
A bunch of horsemen curtly asked his name,
Their leader in a different dialect stated
A war was on for which he was to blame,

And he must help them. The assent he gave
Was founded on desire for self-effacement
In order not to lose his birthright; brave,
For nothing would be easier than replacement,

Which would not give him time to follow further
The details of his own defeat and murder.

Phoenix, October–November 1941 7P, TNS, CP

Observation

Only in books the flat and final happens,
Only in dreams we meet and interlock,
The hand impervious to nervous shock,
The future proofed against our vain suspense;

But since the tideline of the incoming past
Is where we walk, and it is air we breathe,
Remember then our only shape is death
When mask and face are nailed apart at last.

Range-finding laughter, and ambush of tears,
Machine-gun practice on the heart's desires
Speak of a government of medalled fears.

Shake, wind, the branches of their crooked wood,
Where much is picturesque but nothing good,
And nothing can be found for poor men's fires.

18 November 1941. Oxford University Labour Club Bulletin,
22 November 1941 (quoted, with differences of setting
and punctuation, in a letter to J. B. Sutton, 20 November
1948) TS, CP

'O what ails thee, bloody sod'

O what ails thee, bloody sod,
Alone and palely loitering,
The leaves are blowing in the quad
    And no birds sing;
Along the lines of windows spring
The orange lights of cosy fun
The radiogram is whispering,
    The day is done:
Why do you wander at the edge
Of the flat weedless garden's lawn,
Down by the river blows the sedge,
    With none to warm,
Though through the evening comes the cry
Of yearly massacres perform'd
Amid the clash of where and why;
    The question formed
Upon the lips that, kissing, choke,
Sprawling amid the chestnut leaves
That circle lightly for a joke
    Around who grieves.
And this is why I shag alone
In half my creeping days are done
The wind coughs sharply in the stone,
    There is no sun
To light my way to bed: the leaves
Are brown upon the icy tree;
The swallows all have left the eaves
    Silently, silently.

4 *December 1941* (letter to J. B. Sutton) MS

'After the casual growing-up'

After the casual growing-up
Between rick and room, the learning of tricks
To startle and amuse, which, it was told
In the safety of the home, would satisfy the world,
Came the sudden invasion: came the avenging dragon.
In a dozen days the landscape had been shattered:
Most of the family fled beyond recall
From the great shudders that shook birds dead from trees
And snakes that came advancing up the lawn:
Then with strange satisfaction the mallet sank in the clock,
Flames woke in the bookcase with a strangled yelp;
Riding warily through that county, the handful of horsemen
Heard all too often the warning to turn back
And scattered: one was slain by alighting eagle,
Others by falling.

              They did not reach the house
Where like a horse he stood among the flowers
Forcing through floorboard: movement not made there.
Only behind the shut eyes in occasional integration
Came the brief portraits from the private album
With a conjurer's impudence, showing how it happened;
Yet knowing none other than these careless lies
In sunlit accent, thither nosed his wish:
Thither where at least it all was hidden
In clouds of days: the penalty of change,
Whose explosion even then was half expected.

between April and 31 December 1941 TS (as 'Fable'), 7P

[160]

'Sailors brought back strange stories of those lands'

Sailors brought back strange stories of those lands
To thrill professors, who in turn retold
The legend to their sons, until their minds
Could mirror every detail: how the gold
Of sunset spread a path across the sea
To point the travellers [sic] way; the single palm
Guarding the bay that promised ecstasy
On the sand's softness where could tread no harm . . .

Yes, all the maps deceived them: they who raised
The sails of Pity on the sea of Need
Exploring, foundered in a gale of woe:
Splintered their vessels under horror's rock
Amid the tides that savaged to and fro
That generation's wreck.

between April and 31 December 1941 TS, 7P

[161]

Dances in Doggerel

(i)

How can the sunlight entertain
Except upon your window pane?
Or what else can the sky effect
Without the colour you reflect?
Each star would powerdive to the grave
Without the title that you gave,
And birds would leave an empty wood
If you forgot their names for good;
So even more, who justifies
The lamp that never lit your eyes,
The door that never let you in,
The book that you did not begin?
Who can extend a word of grace
To films that do not show your face,
Loudspeakers that your voice distort,
Or gramophones that cut you short?
What value has a word or scene
Except to show where you have been,
And take its formal place upon
The landscape of illusion?

For who by railway leaves behind
Your praising scenery, will find
The sun without a word to say,
The sky to face another way;
The stars will talk together, and
The birds will never be at hand;
The lamp will wonder who you are,
The door will always be ajar,
The book predict an age of woe,
The film a real murder show,
The blind loudspeaker threaten pain,

The gramophone not sing again,
For they become, outside your rule,
A painting by a different school,
A poem in a different tongue,
A song too ghastly to be sung,
Or most of all, a freakish play,
Enacted in broad light of day,
With me upon the blinding stage
At whom the hostile audience rage . . .

(ii)

The longest-running hit of Summer
Lacked a leading character;
Though the settings on the river seemed
Far better than was ever dreamed,
And minor players knew their parts
With songs like arrows to our hearts,
Something still was missing – not
That one could quarrel with the plot –
But it seemed no character would enter
And speak directly from the centre,
Charming all the play's applause,
And being both result and cause
Of every flower and bridge and tree
In their expensive pageantry.
No presence vitalised the cast
That all their normal best surpassed,
Or sung an idiotic verse
With more than usual personal force,
And so production slowly ceased;
The theatre was to Autumn leased,
The wind tore tatters in the wood,
The flowers blew down and lay for good,
Clouds proceeded down the river,
Raindrops made its surface quiver,

The sun charred to a smouldering heap,
Garden turned over in their sleep,
And Autumn's tragic, slight romance
Played to a thinning audience.

Now the old year lies behind
In ashes, and at last I find
One who in slapstick Spring's revue
With beauty could astonish too,
Would star in Summer's loaded masque
As regally as I could ask,
Capture Autumn's slipping grace
By a shadow on the face,
And Winter's classic speech recite
Beneath the moon's frostbitten light;
But now the players have moved on
And happiness has come and gone,
And in a different land I live,
The part no longer mine to give.

between April and 31 December 1941 7P

Lines after Blake

Skies by time are threaded through,
Not stopping to admire the view,
But any scene described can be
A paradise of sympathy;

Do literary memories
Serve to pay the Devil's fees?
And Falsehood's memorable face
Evanescent Truth displace?

If the flower forgets the earth
And the eldest son his birth
There is no place in daylight thought
For what myopic darkness taught.

between April and 31 December 1941 7P

'This was your place of birth, this daytime palace'

This was your place of birth, this daytime palace,
This miracle of glass, whose every hall
The light as music fills, and on your face
Shines petal-soft; sunbeams are prodigal
To show you pausing at a picture's edge
To puzzle out the name, or with a hand
Resting a second on a random page –

The clouds cast moving shadows on the land.

Are you prepared for what the night will bring?
The stranger who will never show his face,
But asks admittance; will you greet your doom
As final; set him loaves and wine; knowing
The game is finished when he plays his ace,
And overturn the table and go into the next room?

Cherwell, 28 February 1942 TS, TNS, CP

[166]

Disintegration

Time running beneath the pillow wakes
Lovers entrained who in the name of love
Were promised the steeples and fanlights of a
    dream;
Joins the renters of each single room
Across the tables to observe a life
Dissolving in the acid of their sex;

Time that scatters hair upon a head
Spreads the ice sheet on the shaven lawn;
Signing an annual permit for the frost
Ploughs the stubble in the land at last
To introduce the unknown to the known
And only by politeness make them breed;

Time over the roofs of what has nearly been
Circling, a migratory, static bird,
Predicts no change in future's lancing shape,
And daylight shows the streets still tangled up;
Time points the simian camera in the head
Upon confusion to be seen and seen.

Oxford University Labour Club Bulletin, February 1942 CP

'I don't like March'

I don't like March;
It's stiff like starch,
And the fucking snow
Doth blow, doth blow;
The wind's fingers
Fasten on strangers
And the heart's dangers
Come and go.

The iron tree
Threatens at me,
And the sky is low
And warns of woe;
Out of a cloud
A voice is heard
Saying aloud:
'Have you killed the snow?'

7 March 1942 (letter to J. B. Sutton) MS

'The doublehanded kiss and the brainwet hatred'

The doublehanded kiss and the brainwet hatred
At noontide marry, and are happy mated;
But the unwarm eye and wish of luck
Bear tears of midnight and come unstuck.

The flesh of love bears both the nail and hammer
Fenced in its brave armour;
But done I spawn the thin sweat on the rose
And the rotten lip and fingers in the salt nose.

March 1942? (letter to J. B. Sutton) MS

'A day has fallen past'

A day has fallen past
    A light flared through my eyes
And sunk; the windy skies
    Show no forecast;

There was sun and wind
    Flowers here and there
Some gardens bare
    Some ruined;

And did I care
    Walking among it?
Was my heart lit
    By the new air?

No, I did as I do
    Every day and night
Drink up the light
    Until I see you.

April 1942 TS

'If days were matches I would strike the lot'

If days were matches I would strike the lot
    Till we met again;
Or if like apples, shake and let them rot,
    The whole crop down;

If hours were poems I would write a book
    To mark our meeting;
Or each a black and crying rook –
    I'd go out shooting;

If minutes were miles between us I would run
    Faster than horses;
Or like dead leaves? The bonfire I would burn
    Would join our faces;

But since all days and hours and minutes grow
    As slow as wheat,
What can my words do, but show
    Them summer heat?

Harry their greenness upward without resting,
    And be the weather
To end this absence with a harvesting
    To reap together?

April 1942 TS, 7COL

'I walk at random through the evening park'

I walk at random through the evening park
The river flows, the tennis courts resound
The children loud upon the playground sing
And in stricter training for the sexual act
Girls and their soldiers pace between the trees.

I walk beneath the sunlit castle walls
The timbered street tilts beautifully down
To reach the taming moat where skiff and punt
Circle giggling from the waterfall
And a professor in the sunset rapes a flower.

I walk among the shut and Sunday shops
See my bent height reflected in a blind
Avoid the pitying curious glances of
The soldiers clattering abreast, and stare
Past the misshapen men and boys in suits.

Along the railinged path between the plots
Of friendly cabbages I hear the trains
See standing all the unconnected trucks
Note the signals down and welcoming
And pause and shiver in the railway arch.

I watch the smoke cough golden in the air
And feel the track curve shining out of sight
And like a swallow cry to travel south
With suitcase packed and one-way tickets punched
Breathless to hear you shouted by the guard
And see your name slide painted into view.

April 1942 TS

'Where should we lie, green heart'

Where should we lie, green heart,
But drowned at summer's foot,
As our arms embroider
Each tall tree shut
In the heat's soundless armour?

How should I speak, but with
Love's many-rooted breath
As a blank bird, or a song
Shaped in the sprung faith
Of this year's southern tongue?

Heart and heart, to nakedness
Unlayered and sewn close,
In this new and blind hour
Sleep defenceless;
Tongues of the year

Unfold through kiss-damp lips
The wound spring shapes;
And the hearts repeat
Every tide's push and lapse
From finish to start.

between April and 10 July 1942 7COL

'I am the latest son'

I am the latest son
Of an ancient family;
In me have crossed again
Their argument and pride,
And all the quality
Of men left better dead;

From one I take my stride
A second wore my smile
My loving from a third
Comes to his bitter end
And stubborn through my will
Another works his mind;

I hold the land they left
Watching as I walk
The robin on the shaft
The spade drawn bright from soil
– Oddments the mind brings back
During the evening stroll

That leads me back to home,
Knowing all the time
That I shall dream their dream,
Tell the lies they told,
And at the end like them
Die as they have died.

between April and 10 July 1942 7COL

[174]

'This triumph ended in the curtained head'

This triumph ended in the curtained head:
The walls blew out and spring remained outside,
Flaring through thick of trees;

Love blew a fuse and saw us in the sun
Nailing the writer's dust against the breeze,
A season and nothing done;

The modern wind runs steady past my ear,
As broken from a broken land I come
Into the furious year

Where hot grass parts the rivers and the roads,
The petrol throne of hoardings and the drum
Of the drought-giving birds.

Here childhood ends, and days again become
The real spread country forcing through my dream.

between April and 10 July 1942 7COL

'The sun swings near the earth'

The sun swings near the earth,
And in his noon-hot breath
Green things break blind and thick
Between the tar and brick.

The railing is tangled in the hedge,
The lawn loses its edge,
And faceless through the hours
Move the stiff shadows of flowers.

Only man feels the sun
As thumbs pressed on his neck; man
Sweats, a bit contemptuous
Of the whole thing, and sleeps in his house.

between April and 10 July 1942 7COL

Leave

There was to be dancing
In the cretonned lounge;
Three kind's of blancmange,
And a cake with icing;

The barrel by the radiogram
Held seven gallons
As a balance
To the seven-pound ham;

They had eggs and butter
Whiskey and chicken
– There wasn't a tradesman
They could have known better.

Hilda was setting the things
In the rose-coloured light;
All the napkins were white
In their silver rings;

She looked at the clock,
Thought his train might be late;
Took a sticky date
Tugged at her frock.

All the family sat round
– Even the dog as well
Thought it was the bell
At every sound:

Father read the leader
Again and again
Queenie and Cousin Pen
Study the carpet border:

Till at last the bell went
At six thirty-four;
Auntie Bee was at the door
Smelling of scent.

Oh what a chatter
As he stood in the hall,
Hung his greatcoat on the wall
And his respirator;

All the months after
His day of service
Fell like grass
At the scythe of their laughter.

Mother got up the dinner
Father forgot the leader
Gave him scotch and soda
And a cheap Corona.

And all they wanted to know –
If an offensive was brewing
All he's been doing
How fast he can go;

Billy asked about
The latest designs:
Auntie Bee: 'How many Huns'
Lights have you put out?'

Uncle Joe: 'Is the pay steady?'
Queenie was intent
On his badge and what it meant –
Then dinner was ready.

They ate till eight;
Course after course
Trifle and tinned asparagus
Piled on his plate;

They drank lime juice and cider
Port and beer
Smoked another cigar
Had another whiskey and soda:

Then Dad got the Rover
An old four-seater
And drove to the theatre
Nine, or over.

Oh how they laughed
At every joke the comic could make
Although Uncle Joe had belly-ache
And hurriedly left.

Then they danced till two-thirty
After a cold supper
Uncle Joe's humour
Approaching the dirty;

Auntie Bee got tight
In dropped Mrs Homer
Got him in a corner
Said it was splendid to fight.

At last, after hours and hours,
Too tired to think
They piled the plates in the sink
And straggled upstairs.

Hilda combed her hair
In their pink double room;
He heard the doom
Of 'Alone at last, dear.'

He had momentary schemes
Of pretending sleep
Then gave up hope –
She lay in his arms.

. . .

The next day dawned fine
But soon filled with clouds
Like dirty great birds:
It began to rain.

He lay all morning in bed
With a hard face;
She did odd jobs in the house
Sullenly, as she always did.

between April and 10 July 1942 7COL

[180]

'As the pool hits the diver, or the white cloud'

As the pool hits the diver, or the white cloud
Gathers the plane scudding through the sky,
You met and married all my weeping world,
And far beyond the harbours where the child
Had played at kissing, all a giant day
Swung me on the logic of your tide.

Calm and burnished, past the year we swam,
Parting the doors of warning soft as grass,
For it was apathy, not love, we feared
Might chain the entrance to the sacred wood,
And separation was a country dance,
A condition of rejoining, when it came.

But on my own in exile all my fears
Watch the landscape in between us grow,
The spawning hills and chimneys thrusting up
Among the roads that tangle off the map
To cheat me if I make a bolt for you,
And lead and lose me through the faceless flowers.

between April and 10 July 1942 TS (as 'Poem'), 7COL

'Flesh to flesh was loving from the start'

Flesh to flesh was loving from the start,
But only to itself, and could not calm
My skeleton of glass that sits and starves,
Nor my marsh hand that sets my music out:

It is not kissing at the acid root
Where my bald spirit found a crying home,
Nor my starved blood that your excitement loves,
And wears all brilliant badged upon your coat:

Yet hand will praise, and skeleton delight,
And root will kiss, and spirit hold you warm,
And blood will call you blood and wear your lives
All red and blue and golden on its heart.

. . .

But you are far away and I have grown
A sack of fever hanging from the sun.

between April and 10 July 1942 TS (as 'Sonnet'), 7COL

July miniatures

The days, torn single from a sketching-block,
With all their scribbles are discarded;
So a mouth went, but for a mistake –
So a face looked, till the day it died –
So, if I could draw it, would be shown
This wind that blows the sky across the field,
And how today the town kneels in the rain.

. . .

If I look till the clouds crack
I shall still see a wet street
And the wet trees along it;
If I think till my heart break
It won't stop the rain
Or my bad life alone.

. . .

Summer has broken up
Fiercely between the hard, defended roads.

Near one of the farms, sunk in the sloping fields,
A bunch of soldiers (on tactical exercise)
Lounge smoking at a gate: they are very still;
Watching two men in shirtsleeves stacking the hay crop;
Above, unnoticed in the sunless skies,
A plane banks in a long descending circle
Preparing to land at the aerodrome, over the hill.

between April and 10 July 1942 7COL

[183]

'Blind through the shouting sun'

Blind through the shouting sun
On the oiled grooves of windy April I run
Crossing the young brink of Spring and Summer's union.

Birds are preaching to the walking pylons
Trying to drown the planes and spraying sirens
And buds preach too, but form their phrase in silence.

The hedge's eager hands stretch green towards me
And I am free
To snap a spray, twist it, gaily or cruelly,

Mock Autumn's collapsing haystacks, as the flowers
Yellow in the graveyard mock the hours
Of the printed dead the downstairs worm devours:

For what pretty thing will come to pass
Is nowhere written in the traceless grass
Nor who lies shot and rotten in the hourglass.

between April and 10 July 1942 7COL

The Returning

They who are slow to forget death's face
Darken our maps like hills, or show
As old stains on the future's laundered cloth;
Another voice speaks under their breath,
Another heart, harder and more slow,
Drives their dry blood; they have lost grace
By sharpened gestures.

                       They avoid some words;
The strident young enthrall and anger them;
For our surface of things
They have a different, shocking set of meanings;
In a recurrent dream
They gather on old battlefields like birds.

between April and 10 July 1942 7COL

Now

O now, as any other spot in time,
Its victim has: the blindly bold, the tame,
The aged – all are ticked off on the list.
The wheel was spun, and these our years have lost;
So we, convicted by the sundial's ban
Of the connived-at sin of being born,
Must by this order pack to travel light
Without the map that always comes too late.

Some say, that only this event will cure
Our tainted plant which needs a drastic care
To bring it to maturity. While some
– Whose ends, perhaps, are even just the same –
Abandon with regret what they were doing
So as to learn the rudiments of dying.

   [*mid-1942?*] TS

Poem: To James Sutton

I hear you are at sea, and at once
In my head the anonymous ship
    Swings like a lamp;
I think of equipment and meals, and the long
Sane hours of a funnel
Against the birdless, interleaving plain.

I stand at the kerb, and hear
The day of shops break over my feet
    In scum the colour of eyes;
I man the helm of the clocks,
Under the cave of my hand the crowd
Wave in the cinema like weed.

For I stand in a shell's porch, wound
On a salting wind that blows
    Sand on the wheels and faces,
And the landless moon lifts over the street,
Calling my loosened fingers from the bay
And long beach of loving.

The land parts and falls. O in my slack heart
The slant of your ship is resurrected,
    The singing and lubber's jokes;
For the seabed of Time is deeper than ten cathedrals,
The route is unridden, and the navigating worm
Hauls me to fear at last.

[*before 17 August 1942*] (included with letter to J. B. Sutton)
TS, AL 14

Fuel Form Blues

Oh see that Fuel Form comin' through the post
Oh see that Fuel Form comin' through the post
It's five weeks late and worse filled up than most.

If your house burns a fire, Lord, you gotta say how
    long,
You gotta put down the merchant that you get it from,
You gotta put it down, and put it down all wrong.

I'd rather be a commando, or drive a railway train,
I'd rather be a commando, Lord! drive a railway train,
Than sort dem Fuel Forms into streets again.

They're large about the blots, the writing's kinda small,
They can spell their own name but that's just all,
Fuckin' Fuel Forms, only thing that I crave,
Fuckin' Fuel Forms, they just won't have,
Fuckin' Fuel Forms, gonna carry me to my grave,
    carry me to my grave.

[*on or before 20 August 1942*] (included with letter to Kingsley
Amis) AL 14

'Llandovery'

Llandovery
Is responsible for the discovery
That semen
Can be produced without women?

[*on or before 20 August 1942*] (included with
letter to Kingsley Amis; the first two lines also
appear in a letter to Amis, 14 July 1942) AL 14

Poem

I met an idiot at a bend in the lane
Who said: I told you not to come here again.
  How tall you're getting. Do you still
  Roll each day away like an iron wheel,
  Making four spokes of food? And I expect the windows
  Want cleaning again, while the mind wanders
  Helpless over the locked hills of others,
  The beautiful rats, farmers, dockyards, mothers,
  Who wear cruelty and kindnesses like rings –
  Or have you put away these things?
  I don't blame you. Someday you'll find all lines
  Lead to a vanished point within the loins;
  (Do you remember the acid used at birth?)
  Time's getting on. Somewhere upon this earth,
  Time's drunken star, the moles have dug your grave;
  One day they'll leave the top off – then who'll save
  The coupons you were cutting out for Life?
  Today death has the last and only laugh.
  But you could change that. Why don't you try?
On each leaf balanced a lighted eye:
Rooks called his words: his body seemed to be
The angle of a strange and single tree.

20 August 1942 TS

'The canal stands through the fields; another'

The canal stands through the fields; another
Year bends in propped-up rows.
The sky is a bird's breast, shielding
Blue shadows in the copse: I see
The burnt moon hanging: feel
The first and faintest premonition:
Autumn, finger on the breath,
A vapoured death.
And yet the novelty I find in death
Is my coincidence; scores
Shiver already in his shaded areas,
Queue for his canteen lunches, live
His ugly camp-life near the villages.
Treat my logic casually, he cries;
And some fall to the trap, hearing
His numbing voice on the ancestral wavelength.
It has all happened so quickly.

Down the other bank, children lie fishing;
Their voices scrape the silence of their hands,
Living unguardedly. What were we doing then?
We walked at evening, tracing
The landscape of ourselves – but this
Had been done for years; we argued, yes;
And yet it seems each sentence threw
A spade of earth, around our lives
Had crept the unforgiving barrenness
That brought the knocking from the bolted door.
– I cannot think what we were doing then:
I cannot fit the broken edge of letters,
The young unfinished days, the faces,
I cannot join them to this Now.
Facts hang a bridle. History.

Ports. Inflation. Even now I shy.
It is not reason, that those kisses
Design a bombsight, those coloured poems
Burn among papers of an enemy consulate.
Yet orders are given, brittle, monstrous:
When did the climate of their utterance
Begin to grow?

           Into lucidity
The moon is focussed, hurtful and important,
Turning already our scene into
A problem of art, and later, pedantry.
The clarified illusion prepares
To invade and colonise. But
It was less simple than that: living
An hour after this sunset meant
More than the fish blipping in the water,
The beauty fractured to suffering, the moths,
The fear, the bewildered gap
Where hope should be; was
A simultaneous exertion on all scales
To grip harmoniously the forward impulse,
Yet still to be aware
Of falling, of mist; the element that lies
Even at the heart of the perceiving instrument.

   23–8 August 1942 TS

[1] A Member of the 1922 Class Looks to the Future

After the war
We shant fight any more
We shall stop making arms
And live on farms

Because when it all ends
We shall all be friends
(Erasing from the memory
Cologne, Coventry)

And it will come to pass
There shall be no lower class
We shall all do what we like
And no one will strike

And Nazi Germany
Shall be set free
And every subject land
Will lick our hand.

– Really, when I foresee
How lovely it will be
In these afteryears,
My eyes fill with tears.

[*late 1942?*] (the first thousand-bomber
raid on Cologne was in May 1942) TS

[2] A Member of the 1922 Class Reads the
1942 Newspapers

After this war
It wont be like it was before:

The word 'enemy'
Will just vanish from our memory.

First of all, Germany
Will be set free,
And every subject land
Will lick our gracious hand.

Then we shall restart work:
No one will shirk
And no one will strike
Because we shall all do what we like.

We shall all become Christians
And ask no questions
For the Church will dispense
'Birth Control and Common Sense.'

Then the miner's eldest son
Will study at Eton
And lounge on French beaches
Sounding his aitches.

We shall be short
Of nothing that can be bought,
So of course we shall be
Perfectly happy.

Indeed, the Millennium
May come,
 Though, considering the facts,
 As rather an anti-climax.

    [*late 1942?*] TS

A Democrat to Others

Fear not, ye conquered hills and plains,
England will remove your chains,
And we shall all live happily
If someone will set England free.

[*late 1942?*] TS

'After a particularly good game of rugger'

After a particularly good game of rugger
A man called me a bugger
Merely because in a loose scrum
I had my cock up his bum.

(quoted in letter to Norman Iles, 8 November 1942) SL

Poem

The camera of the eye
Spools out twelve months; the memory
Spells underneath, how this was snow,
And this was drowned in heat, and this
Derelict, among gulls.
And every tree has told
Death of the drowsed year,
But none of you, or me,
Aleaf, we, living still.

A year of us. And true words cannot speak
Except by accident stuck around the brain,
Chucked from unfinished weeks,
For days can grow
Softly from a stem, and glow,
And fall at last behind a wall
Loosening their sweetness on the earth.
The branch lifts up:
And it is all as though they had not been.
And lives can choose a moment to be born,
Put forth their thickened leaves
Under the light, and live;
And they can draw some sweetness from the earth
Before the month fall down
And bury them as though they had not been.
Words have no lips to kiss them back to life.
Words have no hands to hold their spilled sweetness.

(Larkin note: *Unfinished, circa December, 1942*) TS

'I dreamed of an out-thrust arm of land'

I dreamed of an out-thrust arm of land
Where gulls blew over a wave
That fell along miles of sand;
And the wind climbed up the caves
To tear at a dark-faced garden
Whose black flowers were dead,
And broke round a house we slept in,
A drawn blind and a bed.

I was sleeping, and you woke me
To walk on the chilled shore
Of a night with no memory,
Till your voice forsook my ear
Till your two hands withdrew
And I was empty of tears,
On the edge of a bricked and streeted sea
And a cold hill of stars.

Arabesque, Hilary term 1943 TNS, CP

Mythological Introduction

A white girl lay on the grass
With her arms held out for love;
Her goldbrown hair fell down her face,
And her two lips move:

    See, I am the whitest cloud that strays
    Through a deep sky:
    I am your senses' crossroads,
    Where the four seasons lie.

She rose up in the middle of the lawn
And spread her arms wide;
And the webbed earth where she had lain
Had eaten away her side.

    Arabesque, Hilary term 1943 CP

A Stone Church Damaged by a Bomb

Planted deeper than roots,
This chiselled, flung-up faith
Runs and leaps against the sky,
A prayer killed into stone
Among the always-dying trees;
Windows throw back the sun
And hands are folded in their work at peace,
Though where they lie
The dead are shapeless in the shapeless earth.

Because, though taller the elms,
It forever rejects the soil,
Because its suspended bells
Beat when the birds are dumb,
And men are buried, and leaves burnt
Every indifferent autumn,
I have looked on that proud front
And the calm locked into walls,
I have worshipped that whispering shell.

Yet the wound, O see the wound
This petrified heart has taken,
Because, created deathless,
Nothing but death remained
To scatter magnificence;
And now what scaffolded mind
Can rebuild experience
As coral is set budding under seas,
Though none, O none sees what patterns it is making?

Oxford Poetry 1942–3, June 1943 CP

[200]

Blues

Sometimes I feel like an eagle in the sky,
Sometimes I feel like an eagle in the sky,
Sometimes I feel I'm gonna lay me down and die.
You can't love a woman, if that woman don't love you,
You can't love a woman, if that woman don't love you,
You can't love a woman that don't care what you do.
She gotta want you like whiskey, she gotta need you like
   rain,
She gotta want you like whiskey, she gotta need you like
   rain,
She gotta cry when you leave her, and cry till you come
   back again.

12 July 1943 (letter to J. B. Sutton) MS

'The -er- university of Stockholm -er-'

The -er- university of Stockholm -er-
Presented Jung with a diploma,
Er- I would present Jung
With -ah- DUNG.

28 July 1943 (letter to J. B. Sutton) MS

The False Friend

It's no good standing there and looking haughty:
I'm very cross: I think you've been a beast,
An utter crawling worm, for nearly all the term –
I think you might apologise, at least.
It might interest you to know I heard from Audrey
That Kathleen said that you told Miss LeQuesne
That my liking for French prose was nothing but a pose –
Elspeth, I'll never speak to you again.

Joan always said, she wondered how I stuck you,
And now I see that she was jolly right;
Oh, I know we did our Maths strolling round the garden paths
Until the moon came up, and it was night . . .
But Wenda said that you told her last Christmas,
When we'd promised to send *cards* to Miss LeQuesne,
That the vow you made was broken, 'cos you sent her a BOOK
    TOKEN

– Elspeth, I'll never *speak* to you again.

August–September 1943 TS, TWG

Bliss

In the pocket of my blazer
  Is a purse of silken brown
With ten shillings (from my birthday)
  And my weekly half-a-crown.

In the toolshed by the stable
  Stands my Junior B.S.A.,
See, I leap, I mount, I pedal! –
  And the wind bears me away.

On the left side of the High Street
  W.H. Smith & Son
Have their local branch, and there I'll
  Stop, and lock my bike, and run

Right up to the glass-topped counter:
  'Have you Colonel Stewart's book
Called "Handling Horses"? . . . Yes – behind you –
  It's twelve and six – you needn't look –'

August–September 1943 (a slightly different version
appears in a letter to Kingsley Amis 20 August 1943)
TS, SL, TWG

Femmes Damnées

The fire is ash: the early morning sun
Outlines the patterns on the curtains, drawn
The night before. The milk's been on the step,
The *Guardian* in the letter-box, since dawn.

Upstairs, the beds have not been touched, and thence
Builders' estates and the main road are seen,
With labourers, petrol-pumps, a Green Line bus,
And plots of cabbages set in between.

But the living-room is ruby: there upon
Cushions from Harrods, strewn in tumbled heaps
Around the floor, smelling of smoke and wine,
Rosemary sits. Her hands are clasped. She weeps.

She stares about her: round the decent walls
(The ribbon lost, her pale gold hair falls down)
Sees books and photos: 'Dance'; 'The Rhythmic Life';
Miss Rachel Wilson in a cap and gown.

Stretched out before her, Rachel curls and curves,
Eyelids and lips apart, her glances filled
With satisfied ferocity; she smiles,
As beasts smile on the prey they have just killed.

The marble clock has stopped. The curtained sun
Burns on: the room grows hot. There, it appears,
A vase of flowers has spilt, and soaked away.
The only sound heard is the sound of tears.

August–September 1943 Sycamore Broadsheet 27, 1978 TS, CP, TWG

[205]

Ballade des Dames du Temps Jadis

Tell me, into what far lands   With a sense of
They are all gone, whom I once knew   'old, unhappy,
With tennis-racquets in their hands,   far-off things'.
And gym-shoes, dabbled with the dew?
Many a one danced like a star,
And many a one was proud and gay
Throughout those happy years, that are
So many summer terms away.

Where is Valerie, who led   Lingeringly.
Every tom-boy prank and rag –
Is her hair still golden-red?
Can she still dash like a stag
As she did at hide-and-seek?
And would she still refuse to play
With a rotter or a sneak,
As many summer terms away?

And Julia, with violet eyes,   Wistfully.
Her cool white skin, and sable hair –
Does she still extemporise
On 'The Londonderry Air'?
Does she still want to take the veil
And clothe herself in white and grey?
And be as exquisite and pale
As many summer terms away?

And when we camped on Priory Hill   With a trace of
(That year when Beth was nearly gored) sad humour.
Wenda and Brenda and brown-legged Jill –
Do they remember how it poured?
And how the lamp had got no wick?
And how we tried to sleep on hay
When Sue ate mushrooms and was sick,
So many summer terms away?

[206]

How many names cry on the wind!
Ann, who wore an Aertex shirt,
Patricia, who played Rosalind,
Jean and her little tartan skirt:
How many crushes, chums, and cliques
Recall in this sad roundelay
Those many golden, golden weeks,
So many summer terms away!

With something of
'the monstrous
crying of wind' –
Yeats, of course.

Now the ponies all are dead,
The summer frocks have been outgrown,
The books are changed, beside the bed,
And all the stitches that were sewn
Have been unpicked, and in disgust
The diaries have been thrown away,
And hockey-sticks are thick with dust –
Those summer terms have flown away.

More slowly, but
gathering feeling
for the end.

Ah, tell me, in what fairy-land
Can I meet Jacqueline or June,
Eat lemon-caley from my hand? –
But no: it has all gone too soon,
And Christine, Barbara, and Madge,
Elspeth, Elizabeth, Esmé
Are with my blazer and my badge,
So many summer terms away.

Rising to, and
falling from, an
ecstasy of nostalgia.

ERRATUM:
Line 27 of this poem should of course read:
    'Brenda and Wenda and brown-legged Jill . . .'

August-September 1943 TS, TWG

Holidays

(To all schoolgirls who visit the Shakespeare Memorial Theatre at Stratford-on-Avon, during the season.)

Let's go to Stratford-on-Avon, and see a play!
   Let's pull Pam and Barbara out of their double bed,
Snatch a breakfast, wheel the four bicycles out of the shed,
   And with lunch in the saddle bags, mount and pedal away!

For September is here, and the summer is nearly past;
   There's dew on the blackberries; mist, and the watery sun
Of autumn draw close, the season is almost done . . .
   Ah, pedal, brown legs, for this matinee may be the last!

Who cares what we see? I have been all of them,
   Rosalind, Viola, Portia, Beatrice too,
I have laughed as they laughed, Jessica, Imogen,
   And, like Miranda, have woken in worlds brave and new;

Cleopatra and Juliet – yes, I have loved and died,
   Or, like Desdemona, been slain by a passionate hand;
Ah, pedal, brown legs! on to the magic land,
   To the queue, and the stools, and the shilling to get inside.

September is here, but the leaves still hang and are green,
   The sun still shines, the bees surround the flowers –
For today, then, we can be happy; for these few hours
   Let the curtain go up once more, and the play be seen:

For winter will come, when the wind endlessly grieves
   For all it has lost, the youth, the joy, the pain,
When the last term is over, the theorems forgotten again,
   And we no more to each other than fallen leaves.

August–September 1943 TS, TWG

The School in August

The cloakroom pegs are empty now,
And locked the classroom door,
The hollow desks are dimmed with dust,
And slow across the floor
A sunbeam creeps between the chairs
Till the sun shines no more.

Who did their hair before this glass?
Who scratched 'Elaine loves Jill'
One drowsy summer sewing-class
With scissors on the sill?
Who practised this piano
Whose notes are now so still?

Ah, notices are taken down,
And scorebooks stowed away,
And seniors grow tomorrow
From the juniors today,
And even swimming groups can fade,
Games mistresses turn grey.

August–September 1943 (a variant version appears in
the novel, *Trouble at Willow Gables*) TS, CP, TWG

Fourth Former Loquitur

A group of us have flattened the long grass
Where through the day we watched the wickets fall
Far from the pav. Wenda has left her hat,
And only I remain, now they are gone,
To notice how the evening sun can show
The unsuspected hollows in the field,
When it is all deserted.

                                    Here they lay,
Wenda and Brenda, Kathleen, and Elaine,
And Jill shock-headed and the pockets of
Her blazer full of crumbs, while over all
The sunlight lay like amber wine, matured
By every minute. Here we sprawled barelegged,
And talked of mistresses and poetry,
Shelly and Miss LeQuesne, and heard the tale
Once more of Gwyneth and the garden-rake,
Grass between clear-cut lips, that never yet
Thrilled to the rouge: a schoolbag full of books,
(Todhunter's Algebra – for end of term
Does not mean you can slack) and dusty feet
Bare-toed in sandals – thus we lay, and thus
The filmy clouds drew out like marble veins,
The sun burned on, the great, old whispering trees
Lengthened their shadow over half the pitch:
Deckchairs that the governors had filled
Grew empty, and the final score was hung,
To show for once the Old Girls had been licked.
Ah what remains but night-time and the bats,
This flattened grass, and all the scores to be
Put in the magazine?

                              Be not afraid,
Brenda and Wenda, Kathleen and Elaine

And brown-legged Jill – three years lie at your back
And at your feet, three more:

                              in just a week
The end of term will part us, to the pale
And stuccoed houses we loved so much

Wenda, Brenda, Kathleen and Elaine
Have flattened down the long grass where they've lain,
And brownlegged Jill has left her hat,
For they have gone to laugh and tack with those
Who've played the Old Girls' match out to its close.

August–September 1943 MS, TWG

'All catches alight'

to Bruce Montgomery

All catches alight
At the spread of spring:
Birds crazed with flight
Branches that fling
Leaves up to the light –
Every one thing,
Shape, colour and voice,
Cries out, Rejoice!
   A drum taps: a wintry drum.

Gull, grass and girl
In air, earth and bed
Join the long whirl
Of all the resurrected,
Gather up and hurl
Far out beyond the dead
What life they can control –
All runs back to the whole.
   A drum taps: a wintry drum.

What beasts now hesitate
Clothed in cloudless air,
In whom desire stands straight?
What ploughman halts his pair
To kick a broken plate
Or coin turned up by the share?
What lovers worry much
That a ghost bids them touch?
   A drum taps: a wintry drum.

Let the wheel spin out,
Till all created things
With shout and answering shout

Cast off rememberings;
Let it all come about
Till centuries of springs
And all their buried men
Stand on the earth again.
   A drum taps: a wintry drum.

[*before 21 April 1944*] (quoted in letter to
J. B. Sutton) POW, TNS, CP

'I see a girl dragged by the wrists'

I see a girl dragged by the wrists
Across a dazzling field of snow,
And there is nothing in me that resists.
Once it would not be so;
Once I should choke with powerless jealousies;
But now I seem devoid of subtlety,
As simple as the things I see,
Being no more, no less, than two weak eyes.

There is snow everywhere,
Snow in one blinding light.
Even snow smudged in her hair
As she laughs and struggles, and pretends to fight;
And still I have no regret;
Nothing so wild, nothing so glad as she
Rears up in me,
And would not, though I watched an hour yet.

So I walk on. Perhaps what I desired
– That long and sickly hope, someday to be
As she is – gave a flicker and expired;
For the first time I'm content to see
What poor mortar and bricks
I have to build with, knowing that I can
Never in seventy years be more a man
Than now – a sack of meal upon two sticks.

So I walk on. And yet the first brick's laid.
Else how should two old ragged men
Clearing the drifts with shovels and a spade
Bring up my mind to fever-pitch again?
How should they sweep the girl clean from my heart,
With no more done
Than to stand coughing in the sun,
Then stoop and shovel snow onto a cart?

The beauty dries my throat.
Now they express
All that's content to wear a worn-out coat,
All actions done in patient hopelessness,
All that ignores the silences of death,
Thinking no further than the hand can hold,
All that grows old,
Yet works on uselessly with shortened breath.

Damn all explanatory rhymes!
To be that girl! – but that's impossible;
For me the task's to learn the many times
When I must stoop, and throw a shovelful:
I must repeat until I live the fact
That everything's remade
With shovel and spade;
That each dull day and each despairing act

Builds up the crags from which the spirit leaps
– The beast most innocent
That is so fabulous it never sleeps;
If I can keep against all argument
Such image of a snow-white unicorn,
Then as I pray it may for sanctuary
Descend at last to me,
And put into my hand its golden horn.

[*before 21 April 1944*] (quoted in letter to J. B. Sutton) POW,
TNS, CP

'The moon is full tonight'

The moon is full tonight
And hurts the eyes,
It is so definite and bright.
What if it has drawn up
All quietness and certitude of worth
Wherewith to fill its cup,
Or mint a second moon, a paradise? –
For they are gone from earth.

[1943–4] POW, TNS, CP

'The horns of the morning'

The horns of the morning
Are blowing, are shining,
The meadows are bright
  With the coldest dew;
The dawn reassembles,
Like the clash of gold cymbals
The sky spreads its vans out
  The sun hangs in view.

Here, where no love is,
All that was hopeless
And kept me from sleeping
  Is frail and unsure;
For never so brilliant,
Neither so silent
Nor so unearthly, has
  Earth grown before.

[1943–4] POW, TNS, CP

'I put my mouth'

I put my mouth
Close to running water:
Flow north, flow south,
It will not matter,
It is not love you will find.

I told the wind:
It took away my words:
It is not love you will find,
Only the bright-tongued birds,
Only a moon with no home.

It is not love you will find:
You have no limbs
Crying for stillness, you have no mind
Trembling with seraphim,
You have no death to come.

[1943–4] POW, TNS, ITGOL, CP

'The bottle is drunk out by one'

The bottle is drunk out by one;
At two, the book is shut;
At three, the lovers lie apart,
Love and its commerce done;
And now the luminous watch-hands
Show after four o'clock,
Time of night when straying winds
Trouble the dark.

And I am sick for want of sleep;
So sick, that I can half-believe
The soundless river pouring from the cave
Is neither strong, nor deep;
Only an image fancied in conceit.
I lie and wait for morning, and the birds,
The first steps going down the unswept street,
Voices of girls with scarves around their heads.

[1943–4] POW, TNS, CP

'Love, we must part now: do not let it be'

Love, we must part now: do not let it be
Calamitous and bitter. In the past
There has been too much moonlight and self-pity:
Let us have done with it: for now at last
Never has sun more boldly paced the sky,
Never were hearts more eager to be free,
To kick down worlds, lash forests; you and I
No longer hold them; we are husks, that see
The grain going forward to a different use.

There is regret. Always, there is regret.
But it is better that our lives unloose,
As two tall ships, wind-mastered, wet with light,
Break from an estuary with their courses set,
And waving part, and waving drop from sight.

[1943–4] POW, TNS, CP

[220]

'Morning has spread again'

Morning has spread again
Through every street,
And we are strange again;
For should we meet
How can I tell you that
Last night you came
Unbidden, in a dream?
And how forget
That we had worn down love good-humouredly,
Talking in fits and starts
As friends, as they will be
Who have let passion die within their hearts.
Now, watching the red east expand,
I wonder love can have already set
In dreams, when we've not met
More times than I can number on one hand.

[1943–4] POW, TNS, CP

[221]

'Heaviest of flowers, the head'

Heaviest of flowers, the head
Forever hangs above a stormless bed;
Hands that the heart can govern
Shall be at last by darker hands unwoven;
Every exultant sense
Unstrung to silence –
The sun drift away.

And all the memories that best
Run back beyond this season of unrest
Shall lie upon the earth
That gave them birth.
Like fallen apples, they will lose
Their sweetness at the bruise,
And then decay.

[1943–4] POW, TNS, ITGOL, CP

'So through that unripe day you bore your head'

So through that unripe day you bore your head,
And the day was plucked and tasted bitter,
As if still cold among the leaves. Instead,
It was your severed image that grew sweeter,
That floated, wing-stiff, focused in the sun
Along uncertainty and gales of shame
Blown out before I slept. Now you are one
I dare not think alive: only a name
That chimes occasionally, as a belief
Long since embedded in the static past.

Summer broke and drained. Now we are safe.
The days lose confidence, and can be faced
Indoors. This is your last, meticulous hour,
Cut, gummed; pastime of a provincial winter.

[1943–4] TS (an earlier version, as 'Sonnet: Penelope,
August 1942'), POW, TNS, CP

'What ant crawls behind the picture?'

What ant crawls behind the picture?
Some dull calalier [sic] monotony
Shone with obsolete rust;
Woman and man, two dogs and a horse;
But oh, the fly, and oh, the centipede.
Grin at me, you sheep and cows.
Why are you together on that silly hill?
Where is the cowherd and where the sheperd [sic]?
And where the important worm?
Give gold Grand Guignol,
Shout your largesse to the poor;
Ignoring the bat that flies in your ear.
Black ships sail, moving nowhere,
On an unknown sea,
Spurning the albatross –
Stop it you maniacs, you will die!
The landgirl is riding her piebald bicycle:
No car will run over her dog.

[1943?] TS

'Someone stole a march on the composer'

Someone stole a march on the composer
And substituted dirt for genius;
He was blind and so unwitting –
Non compos till they played it to him.
This was his death-shriek of Infamy:
'Oh, to treat an old man so!'
The theif [sic] merely laughted [sic], and whistled an air –
The very tune he had stolen;
But the old chap never smiled:
He didn't see the joke: he was blind.

[1943?] TS

'Did you hear his prayer, God?'

Did you hear his prayer, God?
Did you sympathise with this poor braggart?
Did you know his shame
In trampling on his pride to petition aid?
You know you did, you monstrous thing;
Your kindness and gentility gave extra ears,
And you kicked him in the teeth to help him on.

[1943?] TS

Leap Year

I saw it smell; I heard it stink.
Whose book review rejuvenated Asia?
A black cat stalking along the sky
With an old man, a lampshade for a hat,
With a brassiere hung from one ear
This was all he had. In place of the other
Grinned a sunken peanut's skull;
Machinegun belts served for his hair,
Two torpedoes for his eyes:
The book he wrote reverberated over Europe.
Marching feet, and a toboggan under his arse,
Two-pennyworth of chips for a brain;
A fivepenny fish dangled before his knees
And the motive power was a tart.
We spat on a pillar box, ran in a vertical street
And vomited along a shop-front;
We hit a bull in the eye, and the Old Man died:
But the book enjoyed a prodigious success.

[1943?] TS

'Some large man had a pendulous eyeball'

Some large man had a pendulous eyeball
That socketed under his ear,
That looked backwards and forwards alike,
And published anything secreted or virginal we had
With imponderable impunity.
How were we safe, we dared not ask;
The fly-paper had us all.
By what unknown effort some brave fellow staggered free
And rushed at the eye with a pin:
Onward David, rush onwards with our bouquet of Hope,
But what avails a flower against a flame?

[1943?] TS

Dawn

To wake, and hear a cock
Out of the distance crying,
To pull the curtains back
And see the clouds flying –
How strange it is
For the heart to be loveless, and as cold as these.

[1943–4] TNS, CP

End

My train draws out, and the last thing I see
Is my three friends turning from the light,
And I am left to travel through the night
With this one thought for company:
Even a king will find himself alone,
Calling for songs one night, old songs, will find
The guests departed, nothing left behind
Except the silence, and a clean-picked bone.

[1943–4?] ts

On Poetry

What have these years brought
But flakes of life?
Sodden ways and thought,
And now, the worst of all,
Love slashed with a knife,
The singing-voice grown gutteral.

Cheapening, worthlessness –
All can be borne
While that voice is dauntless;
But let it once fail
And the hair will be shorn,
The very heart grow pale.

[1943–4?] TS

[231]

Inscription on a Clockface

For this is as it is,
Not beautiful or strong,
In every detail less
Than in its former days –
Let us rejoice, as long
As we have breath to praise.

[1943–4?] TS

'Wall up the day in words'

Wall up the day in words;
Let no quarrelsome branch break loose
Or petalled ignorance be dropped,
And you will have built a statue of bread
To be pecked to death by the birds.

What is it a bird sings?
The encarmining of piebald agonies?
Or none of these things?

[1943–4?] TS

'There is snow in the sky'

There is snow in the sky.
When will it fall down,
That the grey clouds that weigh
Immoveable across the town
Can break, and blow away?
And I accept afresh
This tattered coat of flesh,
These crossed sticks of bone.

[1943–4?] TS

'If I saw the sky in flames'

If I saw the sky in flames
The sky being charred like paper
Each constellation crackling like a thornbush,
I should wish to have lain with women,
Ridden horses to the sea.

When my body fills with death
Like a jar of smoke, like a ship
Lying at last on the seabed –
I shall wish to have lain with women,
Ridden horses to the sea.

[1943–4?] TS

'When this face was younger'

When this face was younger,
    One man and I
Heaped love on each other
    Till love ran dry;
Since mine was the stronger
    Mine is the more pain:
He loves no longer:
    I love not again.

[1943–4?] TS

'Summer extravagances shrink'

Summer extravagances shrink:
And now memories drop
Forsakenly, I used to think,
A finite and a shapely crop,
Nothing was more mistaken:
At the fierce unfinished centre
Everything grows and is broken,
Spring, summer, and winter.

If gulls rose in the wind
Crying, and fell away
From the climbed headland
One similar day
To this, we were lucky but
Can claim no credit,
For nothing consolate
Ever was granted;

And the eye must descend
Through the sparse field of years
To this empty land,
This desert of houses
Although the aristocratic
And to-be-denied
Gold sun throws back
Endless and cloudless pride.

[1943–4?] TS

'Kick up the fire, and let the flames break loose'

Kick up the fire, and let the flames break loose
To drive the shadows back;
Prolong the talk on this or that excuse,
Till the night comes to rest
While some high bell is beating two o'clock.
Yet when the guest
Has stepped into the windy street, and gone,
Who can confront
The instantaneous grief of being alone?
Or watch the sad increase
Across the mind of this prolific plant,
Dumb idleness?

[1943–4] TNS, CP

Winter

In the field, two horses,
Two swans on the river,
While a wind blows over
A waste of thistles
Crowded like men;
And now again
My thoughts are children
With uneasy faces
That awake and rise
Beneath running skies
From buried places.

For the line of a swan
Diagonal on water
Is the cold of winter,
And each horse like a passion
Long since defeated
Lowers its head,
And oh, they invade
My cloaked-up mind
Till memory unlooses
Its brooch of faces –
Streams far behind.

Then the whole heath whistles
In the leaping wind,
And shrivelled men stand
Crowding like thistles
To one fruitless place;
Yet still the miracles
Exhume in each face
Strong silken seed,
That to the static

Gold winter sun throws back
Endless and cloudless pride.

[1943–4] TNS, ITGOL, CP

'Like the train's beat'

Like the train's beat
Swift language flutters the lips
Of the Polish airgirl in the corner seat.
The swinging and narrowing sun
Lights her eyelashes, shapes
Her sharp vivacity of bone.
Hair, wild and controlled, runs back:
And gestures like these English oaks
Flash past the windows of her foreign talk.

The train runs on through wilderness
Of cities. Still the hammered miles
Diversify behind her face.
And all humanity of interest
Before her angled beauty falls,
As whorling notes are pressed
In a bird's throat, issuing meaningless
Through written skies; a voice
Watering a stony place.

[1943–4] TNS, CP

The Dancer

Butterfly
Or falling leaf,
Which ought I to imitate
In my dancing?

And if she were to admit
The world weaved by her feet
Is leafless, is incomplete?
And if she abandoned it,
Broke the pivoted dance,
Set loose the audience?
Then would the moon go raving,
The moon, the anchorless
Moon go swerving
Down at the earth for a catastrophic kiss.

[1943–4] TNS, CP

'To write one song, I said'

To write one song, I said,
As sad as the sad wind
That walks around my bed,
Having one simple fall
As a candle-flame swells, and is thinned,
As a curtain stirs by the wall
– For this I must visit the dead.
Headstone and wet cross,
Paths where the mourners tread,
A solitary bird,
These call up the shade of loss,
Shape word to word.

That stones would shine like gold
Above each sodden grave,
This, I had not foretold,
Nor the birds' clamour, nor
The image morning gave
Of more and ever more,
As some vast seven-piled wave,
Mane-flinging, manifold,
Streams at an endless shore.

[1943–4] TNS, CP

[243]

Ugly Sister

I will climb thirty steps to my room,
Lie on my bed;
Let the music, the violin, cornet and drum
Drowse from my head.

Since I was not bewitched in adolescence
And brought to love,
I will attend to the trees and their gracious silence,
To winds that move.

[1943–4] TNS, CP

'One man walking a deserted platform'

One man walking a deserted platform;
Dawn coming, and rain
Driving across a darkening autumn;
One man restlessly waiting a train
While round the streets the wind runs wild,
Beating each shuttered house, that seems
Folded full of the dark silk of dreams,
A shell of sleep cradling a wife or child.

Who can this ambition trace,
To be each dawn perpetually journeying?
To trick this hour when lovers re-embrace
With the unguessed-at heart riding
The winds as gulls do? What lips said
Starset and cockcrow call the dispossessed
On to the next desert, lest
Love sink a grave round the still-sleeping head?

[1944] (a slightly different version is quoted in a letter to
J. B. Sutton, 8 October 1944) TNS, ITGOL (as 'Getaway'), CP, SL

'If hands could free you, heart'

If hands could free you, heart,
   Where would you fly?
Far, beyond every part
Of earth this running sky
Makes desolate? Would you cross
City and hill and sea,
   If hands could set you free?

I would not lift the latch;
   For I could run
Through fields, pit-valleys, catch
All beauty under the sun –
Still end in loss:
I should find no bent arm, no bed
   To rest my head.

[1943–4] TNS, CP

'This is the first thing'

This is the first thing
I have understood:
Time is the echo of an axe
Within a wood.

[1943–4] TNS, CP

'Is it for now or for always'

Is it for now or for always,
The world hangs on a stalk?
Is it a trick or a trysting-place,
The woods we have found to walk?

Is it a mirage or miracle,
Your lips that lift at mine:
And the suns like a juggler's juggling-balls,
Are they a sham or a sign?

Shine out, my sudden angel,
Break fear with breast and brow,
I take you now and for always,
For always is always now.

[1943–4] TNS, CP

'Pour away that youth'

Pour away that youth
That overflows the heart
Into hair and mouth;
Take the grave's part,
Tell the bone's truth.

Throw away that youth
That jewel in the head
That bronze in the breath;
Walk with the dead
For fear of death.

[1943–4] TNS, CP

Girl Saying Goodbye

How she must feel the frailty
Of mouth on mouth!
How all she knew at night
Is lost in the light!

Starstrong, the wheels begin to move:
And this is all the loyalty
Earth can show on earth.
She can show no more love.

c. 21 April 1944 (air letter to J. B. Sutton) TS

'Mary Cox in tennis socks'

Mary Cox in tennis socks
   Mary Cox in shorts
Teacups tinkling in the breeze
Tables underneath the trees
And Mary Cox with suntanned knees
   In tennis socks and shorts.

Verse II

White lines drawn across the lawn
   And Mary Cox in shorts
Jug and glasses in the shade
Lilac trees and lemonade
Racquet-presses carefully laid
   Beside the tennis-courts.

Verse III

But Summer dies and Summer skies
   Grow cloudy in my thoughts
Yet still as in a crystal creeps
The shadow of a rose that sleeps
And Mary Cox's shadow leaps
   In tennis socks and shorts.

1 July 1944 MS

Nursery Tale

All I remember is
The horseman, the moonlit hedges,
The hoofbeats shut suddenly in the yard,
The hand finding the door unbarred:
And I recall the room where he was brought,
Hung black and candlelit; a sort
Of meal laid out in mockery; for though
His place was set, there was no more
Than one unpolished pewter dish, that bore
The battered carcase of a carrion crow.

So every journey that I make
Leads me, as in the story he was led,
To some new ambush, to some fresh mistake:
So every journey I begin foretells
A weariness of daybreak, spread
With carrion kisses, carrion farewells.

August 1944 TS, TNS, CP

'Small paths lead away'

Small paths lead away
From the fence round the wood,
Small animals prey
Where no foot ever trod;
Smoke leans from unseen fires
In many villages,
Where wet leaves and briars
Burn behind cottages.

There are more fruits, more flowers
Than one hand can pick,
More trembling hours,
More eyes, more music
Than one slow traveller
Ever can meet,
Though bright illusion spur
His credulous feet.

29 August 1944 TS

'If grief could burn out'

If grief could burn out
Like a sunken coal,
The heart would rest quiet,
The unrent soul
Be still as a veil;
But I have watched all night

The fire grow silent,
The grey ash soft:
And I stir the stubborn flint
The flames have left,
And grief stirs, and the deft
Heart lies impotent.

5 October 1944 (quoted in letter to
J. B. Sutton, 8 October 1944) WKBK, TNS, CP, SL

'Sheaves under the moon in ghostly fruitfulness'

Sheaves under the moon in ghostly fruitfulness
Cold berries in the hedge, flowers rank in seed,
The many leaves that die, but find no rest,
All journey down towards forgetfulness,
Towards death, ages of deathly autumns spread
Across the land, seeming a white mist,

I see them as a robe the year puts on
Against the sharpening stars, the incarnate year
Displayed, as if in evidence winter demands
Of life filled up to brimming. And the sun
Draws off from autumn in a kind of fear:
I am ashamed to face death with empty hands.

6 October 1944 WKBK

'Within the dream you said'

Within the dream you said:
Let us kiss then,
In this room, in this bed,
But when all's done
We must not meet again.

Hearing this last word,
There was no lambing-night,
No gale-driven bird
Nor frost-encircled root
As cold as my heart.

12 October 1944 WKBK, TNS, ITGOL, CP

Night-Music

At one the wind rose,
And with it the noise
Of the black poplars.

Long since had the living
By a thin twine
Been led into their dreams
Where lanterns shine
Under a still veil
Of falling streams;
Long since had the dead
Become untroubled
In the light soil.
There were no mouths
To drink of the wind,
Nor any eyes
To sharpen on the stars'
Wide heaven-holding,
Only the sound
Long sibilant-muscled trees
Were lifting up, the black poplars.

And in their blazing solitude
The stars sang in their sockets through the night:
'Blow bright, blow bright
The coal of this unquickened world.'

12 *October 1944* WKBK, TNS, ITGOL, CP

'Climbing the hill within the deafening wind'

Climbing the hill within the deafening wind
The blood unfurled itself, was proudly borne
High over meadows where white horses stood;
Up the steep woods it echoed like a horn
Till at the summit under shining trees
It cried: Submission is the only good;
Let me become an instrument sharply stringed
For all things to strike music as they please.

How to recall such music, when the street
Darkens? Among the rain and stone places
I find only an ancient sadness falling,
Only hurrying and troubled faces,
The walking of girls' vulnerable feet,
The heart in its own endless silence kneeling.

23 October 1944 WKBK, TNS, CP

The North Ship

Legend

I saw three ships go sailing by,
Over the sea, the lifting sea,
And the wind rose in the morning sky,
And one was rigged for a long journey.

The first ship turned towards the west,
Over the sea, the running sea,
And by the wind was all possessed
And carried to a rich country.

The second turned towards the east,
Over the sea, the quaking sea,
And the wind hunted it like a beast
To anchor in captivity.

The third ship drove towards the north,
Over the sea, the darkening sea,
But no breath of wind came forth,
And the decks shone frostily.

The northern sky rose high and black
Over the proud unfruitful sea,
East and west the ships came back
Happily or unhappily:

But the third went wide and far
Into an unforgiving sea
Under a fire-spilling star,
And it was rigged for a long journey.

8 October 1944 (a slightly different version is included in a
letter to J. B. Sutton, 8 October 1944) WKBK, TNS, CP, SL

Songs
65°N

My sleep is made cold
By a recurrent dream
Where all things seem
Sickeningly to poise
On emptiness, on stars
Drifting under the world.

When waves fling loudly
And fall at the stern,
I am wakened each dawn
Increasingly to fear
Sail-stiffening air,
The birdless sea.

Light strikes from the ice:
Like one who near death
Savours the serene breath,
I grow afraid,
Now the bargain is made,
That dream draws close.

27 October 1944 WKBK, TNS, CP

70°N
Fortunetelling

'You will go a long journey,
In a strange bed take rest,
And a dark girl will kiss you
As softly as the breast
Of an evening bird comes down
Covering its own nest.

'She will cover your mouth
Lest memory exclaim
At her bending face,
Knowing it is the same
As one who long since died
Under a different name.'

2 November 1944 WKBK, TNS, CP

75°N
Blizzard

Suddenly clouds of snow
Begin assaulting the air,
As falling, as tangled
As a girl's thick hair.

Some see a flock of swans,
Some a fleet of ships
Or a spread winding-sheet,
But the snow touches my lips

And beyond all doubt I know
A girl is standing there
Who will take no lovers
Till she winds me in her hair.

29 *October 1944* WKBK, TNS, CP

Above 80°N

A woman has ten claws,
Sang the drunken boatswain;
Farther than Betelgeuse,
More brilliant than Orion
Or the planets Venus and Mars,
The star flames on the ocean;
'A woman has ten claws,'
Sang the drunken boatswain.

   31 October 1944 WKBK, TNS, CP

'Why should I be out walking'

Why should I be out walking
On the night of the high wind?
Why should I understand
The trees in their talking?
Because I have had no lover
Since love ran dry
When this face was younger
This wind was high.

9 November 1944 WKBK

'Snow has brought the winter to my door'

Snow has brought the winter to my door:
Walking among its scraps I try to fix
Afresh what symbols I have used before
But find them shrunk like snowdrifts in a thaw
Of less account than heaps of broken sticks.

Time runs like water underneath the ice,
Runs on above high cloud, until it bring
Ruin on to winter's ceremonies
Disordering the frost no less than these
Past emblems, split and buried in last spring.

They with their going leave no power at all,
Or I would summon up new imagery
As supple as the rooks that rise and fall
Over these northern fields: but I can call
No mortal birds down to a barren tree.

8 January 1945 WKBK (torn-out page), AL 11

For My Father

Because there is no housing from the wind,
No health in winter, and no permanence
Except in the inclement grave,
Among the littering alien snow I crave
The gift of your courage and indifference.

13 *January 1945* WKBK (torn-out page), AL 11

'Because the images would not fit'

Because the images would not fit
Of silent instrument, unplenteous horn,
Alone in the deserted street
I walked, till suddenly on the wind
A chill heresy was borne.
'No wishing in your starveling heart
Nor choice of unharmonious mind
Brought you in these great riches any part.'

14 January 1945 WKBK (two versions deleted in WKBK, dated 13.1.45 and 14.1.45)

'Days like a handful of grey pearls'

Days like a handful of grey pearls
Go past me, savourless and cold;
Among the many hours and miles,
Among the many faces, only one
Was happy – that, a woman, old,
Witless, counting her fingers in the sun.

The winter seems too great a load to move,
And fantasies of spring to house
Deeply in caverns with outmoded love;

Dreams before daybreak cannot keep
Their essences, or surely I should rouse
Into a dawn where all that's past seems sleep.

16 January 1945 WKBK, TS

'Numberless blades of grass'

Numberless blades of grass
And only one thin blade
That is the moon.

                                   I have made
As many promises
As there are grasses frightened by the wind
In lonely fields, promises enough
Till eyes applauded, yet turned further off,
Unsatisfied with words. In this I was blind.
Such promises have not proved durable:
Breath is as well spent praying to the moon.

Blade of the moon drop down:
Harvest my spent grasses. Come to the full.

19 January 1945 WKBK

Beggars

The mangers are all chaff:
Wind claps about the fields
Frightening thin birds –
There is not corn enough;
    The black cowl and the white cowl
    Never show us their faces.

Rats scuttle in the barn,
Sheep crowd beneath the hedge:
Soldiers are on the march
And the dogs off the chain;
    The black cowl and the white cowl
    Never show us their faces.

Though we beg for hours
Where the high-roads cross,
No living thing will pass:
All are within doors;
    The black cowl and the white cowl
    Never show us their faces.

I have loaded my soul
With a maledictus,
For beef and a big house
Would help it on to Hell –
    The black cowl and the white cowl
    Never show us their faces.

5.2.45 and 6.10.46 WKBK, TS

'Draw close around you'

'Draw close around you
Your courage and your love
Lest the winter find you
Helpless, lest you have
No coals nor kindling sticks
Built up against what time
The iron cloud breaks,
And winter rages round one narrow room.'

Was I so scant of these
That, for a word of love
Said among lengthening days,
I have nothing to give?
Did winter so envenom
Its beaten grappling
That love cannot assume
The racing approach of spring?

   14 February 1945 WKBK

Quatrain

I have despatched so many words
Against the sun, that now, like homing birds
Each carrying its separate branch of pain,
Heavily they gather at my heart again.

26 February 1945 WKBK, 2 TS

'Where was this silence learned'

Where was this silence learned,
Heart, whose one care it was
To wall each day up in words?
Wind does not rage the less
Along the hillside grass,
Nor are the common birds
Less delicate of feather
Than when such sights could rouse
Proud music on your part.
Can it be that, whether
Solicited or not,
The cold face never turned?

27 February 1945 WKBK, 2 TS

'Coming at last to night's most thankful springs'

Coming at last to night's most thankful springs,
I meet a runner's image, sharply kept
Ambered in memory from mythology;
A man who never turned aside and slept,
Nor put on masks of love; to whom all things
Were shadowlike against the news he bore,
Pale as the sky: one who for certainty
Had not my hesitations, lest he see
The loud and precious scroll of sounding shields
Not worth the carrying, when held before
The full moon travelling through her shepherdless fields.

1 March 1945 WKBK, TS, ITGOL, CP

[274]

'Ride with me down into the spring'

Ride with me down into the spring
For the long secret roots have woven
Everything into a ritual,
And you, whose face throughout the months has grown
To something nearly tangible,
Can mingle with it like a living thing.

All beauty that the winter bears
Was laid like shadows on your brow
That your gentleness should not be
Shamed by this meeting: now
I would bring you to the ceremony.
Why do you stand so, letting fall these tears?

16 March 1945 WKBK

'Safely evening behind the window'

Safely evening behind the window
Falls, and the fresh trees have drowsed,
Trees, which at noonday stood amazed
At a loud bird breaking from a furrow,
Wheeling, falling, crying above the nest
So dark-earth-cradled, lost with its own shadow.

Yet your beauty, startled from my heart,
Went to no exile. This I had not loved
Till I had seen it laugh and be unmoved
At my praises – having no part in it.

11 April 1945 WKBK

'When trees are quiet, there will be no more weeping'

When trees are quiet, there will be no more weeping,
But their distress is long; and when the wind
Dies out, all the now-wakeful will be sleeping:
Let that hour come, when silent clocks turn blind
The speculating stars, when the strings' quest
Strives to a halt, and all this pain makes end,
And all my thoughts an unpredicted rest.

27 April 1945 WKBK (torn-out page), 2 TS, AL 11

Song with a Spoken Refrain

'Do not tie my love,
And yours shall go free,
When I am disfavoured,
Do not love me,
Above all else I hate
Love out of charity.'
And this was said in a confident voice.

'I love you well enough,
But being cold
I have no need of love –
And I am told
Love does distress the young
And plague the old.'
And this was said in a confident voice.

10 June 1945 WKBK, TS

Plymouth

A box of teak, a box of sandalwood,
A brass-ringed spyglass in a case,
A coin, leaf-thin with many polishings,
Last kingdom of a gold forgotten face,
These lie about the room, and daily shine
When new-built ships set out towards the sun.

If they had any roughness, any flaw,
An unfamiliar scent, all this has gone;
They are no more than ornaments, or eyes,
No longer knowing what they looked upon,
Turned sightless; rivers of Eden, rivers of blood
Once blinded them, and were not understood.

The hands that chose them rust upon a stick.
Let my hands find such symbols, that can be
Unnoticed in the casual light of day,
Lying in wait for half a century
To split chance lives across, that had not dreamed
Such coasts had echoed, or such seabirds screamed.

25 June 1945, Mandrake, May 1946, WKBK, TS, ITGOL, CP

'Happiness is a flame'

Happiness is a flame
Balanced upon the tip
Of the flight of moving days.
Where does its strength come?
Is it drawn out of sleep,
From loyalty of friends,
Or out of drunkenness,
Dreams and long-spun pretence?
Is it a faith that burns?
Or is it no more than sense
Of outlays and returns,
Work of our many hands?

These compass, at the best,
As much as an idiot could,
Who, at the height of June,
Sets out to reach the sun,
Taking the first road
That promises the West.
Friends feel and speak disgust
When all else has [*sic*] felt and spoken;
Sleep gives more ground to death;
And can it be called faith,
Proud every bone is broken?
While years in that leprous bed,
Pillowed with fantasy, must
Lay sickness upon the mouth.

All these man loses, yet
The flame does not lose its height:
Bankrupt in front of death
Dreams, friends and sleep blow free,
Free generation's thread,
And all the rational joys

Fall broken-winged; and he
Who sought for the mystery
Finds at the finish this:
    'Happiness rests upon
    Devoutness of the blood.
    Rich oil of youth and strength
    Soon passes, and at length
    Has nothing of what it would;
    Then, when its power is gone,
    It learns to fall and rise
    As the sun, as the sea of grass,
    As the ocean of whispering leaves,
    Through numberless births and graves.'

[*June 1945?*] WKBK, TS

[281]

'Lie with me, though the night return outside'

Lie with me, though the night return outside.
Wind changes weathercocks: would it could change
Me to a bridegroom, you into a bride,
And this our world, painful and dull and strange,
Back to its innocence.

               But now the rain
Falls steadily on young, half-ripened corn,
And we have missed our summer. Not again
Can love cast storms back in the teeth of storms.

2 July 1945 WKBK, 2 TS

'The dead are lost, unravelled; but if a voice'

The dead are lost, unravelled; but if a voice
Could shake them back, reshape each sunless bone
To cage a mind, and offer them a choice
Of painful walking on the earth again,
Or, once more, death – how their sad eagerness
Would beat against this life! Even that breath
They fought to catch an hour before their death
Would fire their lungs with too much happiness.

Cries in the street, the slam of a broken door,
Windows of fog, black wheeltracks in the snow –
All would enchant them. But what can the dead give?
Such knowledge has no words: it comes before
The second when life drops them, and they know
The golden quality of things that live.

23 *August 1945* (the first five and a half lines are quoted in a letter
to Kingsley Amis, 22 August 1945) WKBK, TS

'Lift through the breaking day'

Lift through the breaking day,
   Wind that pursues the dawn:
Under night's heedless stone
Houses and river lay –
   Now to the east they shine.

Climb the long summer hills
   Where the wide trees are spread,
Drown the cold-shadowed wood
With noise of waterfalls;
   And under chains of cloud

Fly on towards the sea:
   Sing there upon the beach
Till all's beyond death's reach,
And empty shells reply
   That all things flourish.

27 August 1945 WKBK, TS, ITGOL, CP

'When the tide draws out'

When the tide draws out
The wreck emerges;
A seabird drifts about,
And sometimes perches
There on the shapeless hull
To make unsettling cries –
Voice of a drowned soul in disguise,
Come nightly to lament like a grey gull.

All day the hull bisects
The waves that travel at shore,
Until the eye accepts
Illusion that it moves once more:
Filled with the desperation of the dead
It seems to press
Out to the west, out towards loneliness –
Till I grow sickened, and must turn my head.

I had thought life would move,
Above the years incredibly take wing;
All by a sudden flight to prove
Slack folded hands bring everything,
Bring sails, that in the morning come to the full,
The wind transfiguring the endless waters
Out of all knowledge: but no minute stirs,
No day mounts up to follow the grey gull.

9/9/45, 23/9/45 (corrected 6/10/46) WKBK, TS (with holograph corrections)

'The cry I would hear'

The cry I would hear
Is not in the wind,
Is not of birds,
Nor the dry sound
Sadness can strike
Off the fruitful air.
In a trap's teeth
What are the words
That break in a shriek,
That break against death?

24 October 1945 WKBK (crossed out)

Portrait

Her hands intend no harm:
Her hands devote themselves
To sheltering a flame;
Winds are her enemies,
And everything that strives
To bring her cold and darkness.

But wax and wick grow short:
These she so dearly guards
Despite her care die out;
Her hands are not strong enough
Her hands will fall to her sides
And no wind will trouble to break her grief.

7 November 1945 Mandrake, May 1946, WKBK, TS, ITGOL (as 'The quiet one'), CP

'Past days of gales'

Past days of gales
When skies are colourless
The acorn falls,
Dies; so for this space
Autumn is motionless.

Because the sun
So hesitates in this decay,
I think we still could turn,
Speak to each other in a different way;
For ways of speaking die,

And yet the sun pardons our voices still,
And berries in the hedge
Through all the nights of rain have come to the full,
And death seems like long hills, a range
We ride each day towards, and never reach.

17 November 1945 WKBK, TS, ITGOL, CP

'Who whistled for the wind, that it should break'

Who whistled for the wind, that it should break
Gently, on this air?
On what ground was it gathered, where
For the carrying, for its own sake,
Is night so gifted?

           Mind never met
Image of death like this, and yet
(All winds crying for that unbroken field,
Day having lifted)
Black flowers burst out wherever the night has knelt.

15 December 1945 WKBK, ITGOL, CP

Going

There is an evening coming in
Across the fields, one never seen before,
That lights no lamps.

Silken it seems at a distance, yet
When it is drawn up over the knees and breast
It brings no comfort.

Where has the tree gone, that locked
Earth to the sky? What is under my hands,
That I cannot feel?

What loads my hands down?

February? 1946 WKBK, ITGOL (as 'Dying Day'), XX, TLD, CP

Deep Analysis

I am a woman lying on a leaf;
  Leaf is silver, my flesh is golden,
Comely at all points, but I became your grief
  When you would not listen.

Through your one youth, whatever you pursued
  So singly, that I would be,
Desiring to kiss your arms and your straight side
  – Why would you not let me?

Why would you never relax, except for sleep,
  Face turned at the wall,
Denying the downlands, wheat, and the white sheep?
  And why was all

Your body sharpened against me, vigilant,
  Watchful, when all I meant
Was to make it bright, that it might stand
  Burnished before my tent?

I could not follow your wishes, but I know
  If they assuaged you
It would not be crying in this dark, your sorrow,
  It would not be crying, so

That my own heart drifts and cries, having no death
  Because of the darkness,
Having only your grief under my mouth
  Because of the darkness.

April 1946 WKBK, ITGOL, CP

'Sky tumbles, the sea'

Sky tumbles, the sea
    Exhausts its tides:
All that they bring
    Is a salt living.

Why do you think love
    Washes up diamonds?
What does a kiss put
    Into empty hands?

Would you wear a shell necklace,
    Sleep under a boat,
Wait winter after winter,
    Nothing but wait?

26 April 1946 WKBK, TS

[292]

'Come then to prayers'

Come then to prayers
And kneel upon the stone,
For we have tried
All courages on these despairs,
And are required lastly to give up pride,
And the last difficult pride in being humble.

Draw down the window-frame
That we may be unparted from the darkness,
Inviting to this house
Air from a field, air from a salt grave,
That questions if we have
Concealed no flaw in this confessional,
And, being satisfied,
Lingers, and troubles, and is lightless,
And so grows darker, as if clapped on a flame,
Whose great extinguishing still makes it tremble.

Only our hearts go beating towards the east.
Out of this darkness, let the unmeasured sword
Rising from sleep to execute or crown
Rest on our shoulders, as we then can rest
On the outdistancing, all-capable flood
Whose brim touches the morning. Down
The long shadows where undriven the dawn
Hunts light into nobility, arouse us noble.

13 May 1946 WKBK, ITGOL, CP

'Sting in the shell'

Sting in the shell
By a blade beaten
To milk-white excitement
Resign torment
And into a pattern
Come still, still.

Your ringing, rage
Up the stinging track,
Out races my carried
Argument – that married
Ten faces back
Unsiring age.

14 May 1946 WKBK

The point of a stick

A stick's-point, drawn
Down a pool's clear bed,
Conjures a sand-cloud
Boiling without sound,
And yet defined
Sharply as the desire your parts have sown.

30/5–3/6/46 WKBK (torn-out page), TS

'There is no clearer speaking'

There is no clearer speaking
Than a bird places on the light
This level evening.
The building of thick tongues
Is stilled, and I am called
To hesitate again towards the unbuilt
Mansions. Beyond the tenderest songs,
What proud undominating flock
Of graces chose this one unspelling beak?

12 June 1946 TS

'And the wave sings because it is moving'

And the wave sings because it is moving;
Caught in its clear side, we also sing.

We are borne across graves, together, apart, together,
In the lifting wall imprisoned and protected,
And so devised to make ourselves unhappy.
Apart, we think we wish ourselves together,
Yet sue for solitude upon our meetings,
Till the unhindered turning of the sea
Changes our comforts into griefs greater
Than they were raised to cancel, breaking them.

Such are the sorrows that we search for meaning,
Such are the cries of birds across the waters,
Such are the mists the sun attacks at morning,
Laments, tears, wreaths, rocks, all ridden down
By the shout of the heart continually at work
To break with beating all our false devices;
Silver-tongued like a share it ploughs up failure,
Carries the night and day, fetches
Profit from sleep, from skies, driven or star-slung,
From all but death takes tithes,
Finds marrow in all but death to feed
And frame to us, but death it cannot invoke.

Death is a cloud alone in the sky with the sun.
Our hearts, turning like fish in the green wave,
Grow quiet in its shadow. For in the word death
There is nothing to grasp; nothing to catch or claim;
Nothing to adapt the skill of the heart to, skill
In surviving, for death it cannot survive,
Only resign the irrecoverable keys.
The wave falters and drowns. The coulter of joy

Breaks. The harrow of death
Deepens. And there are thrown up waves.

And the waves sing because they are moving.
And the waves sing above a cemetery of waters.

14 September 1946 WKBK (torn-out page), ITGOL, CP

Two Guitar Pieces

I

The tin-roofed shack by the railroad
Casts a shadow. Wheatstraws in the white dust
And a wagon standing. Stretched out into the sun
A dozen legs are idle in dungarees,
Dark hands and heads shaded from sun and working.
One frowns above a guitar: the notes, random
From tuning, wander into the heat
Like a new insect chirping in the scrub,
Untired at noon. A chord gathers and spills,
And a southern voice tails out around one note
Contentedly discontent.

                Though the tracks
Burn to steel cities, they are taking
No one from these parts. Anyone could tell
Not even the wagon aims to go anywhere.

II

I roll a cigarette, and light
A spill at the stove. With a lungful of smoke
I join you at the window that has no curtain;
There we lean on the frame, and look
Below at the platz. A man is walking along
A path between the wreckage. And we stare at the dusk,
Sharing the cigarette.

                Behind us, our friend
Yawns, and collects the cards. The pack is short,
And dealing from now till morning would not bring
The highest hands. Besides, it's too dark to see.
So he kicks the stove, and lifts the guitar to his lap,
Strikes this note, that note.

I am trembling:
I am suddenly charged with their language, these six strings,
Suddenly made to see they can declare
Nothing but harmony, and may not move
Without a happy stirring of the air
That builds within this room a second room;
And the accustomed harnessing of grief
Tightens, because together or alone
We cannot trace that room; and then again
Because it is not a room, nor a world, but only
A figure spun on stirring of the air,
And so, untrue.

           And so, I watch the square,
Empty again, like hunger after a meal.
You offer the cigarette and I say, Keep it,
Liking to see the glimmer come and go
Upon your face. What poor hands we hold,
When we face each other honestly! And now the guitar again,
Spreading me over the evening like a cloud,
Drifting, darkening: unable to bring rain.

15 and 18 September 1946 WKBK, ITGOL, CP

The Dedicated

Some must employ the scythe
Upon the grasses,
That the walks be smooth
For the feet of the angel.
Some keep in repair
The locks, that the visitor
Unhindered passes
To the innermost chamber.

Some have for endeavour
To sign away life
As lover to lover,
Or a bird using its wings
To fly to the fowler's compass,
Not out of willingness,
But being aware of
Eternal requirings.

And if they have leave
To pray, it is for contentment
If the feet of the dove
Perch on the scythe's handle,
Perch once, and then depart
Their knowledge. After, they wait
Only the colder advent,
The quenching of candles.

18 September 1946 WKBK, ITGOL (untitled), XX, CP

Wedding-Wind

The wind blew all my wedding-day,
And my wedding-night was the night of the high wind;
And a stable door was banging, again and again,
That he must go and shut it, leaving me
Stupid in candlelight, hearing rain,
Seeing my face in the twisted candlestick,
Yet seeing nothing. When he came back
He said the horses were restless, and I was sad
That any man or beast that night should lack
The happiness I had.

                 Now in the day
All's ravelled under the sun by the wind's blowing.
He has gone to look at the floods, and I
Carry a chipped pail to the chicken-run,
Set it down, and stare. All is the wind
Hunting through clouds and forests, thrashing
My apron and the hanging cloths on the line.
Can it be borne, this bodying-forth by wind
Of joy my actions turn on, like a thread
Carrying beads? Shall I be let to sleep
Now this perpetual morning shares my bed?
Can even death dry up
These new delighted lakes, conclude
Our kneeling as cattle by all-generous waters?

26 September 1946 WKBK, ITGOL, XX, TLD, CP

Träumerei

In this dream that dogs me I am part
Of a silent crowd walking under a wall,
Leaving a football match, perhaps, or a pit,
All moving the same way. After a while
A second wall closes on our right,
Pressing us tighter. We are now shut in
Like pigs down a concrete passage. When I lift
My head, I see the walls have killed the sun,
And light is cold. Now a giant whitewashed D
Comes on the second wall, but much too high
For them to recognise: I await the E,
Watch it approach and pass. By now
We have ceased walking and travel
Like water through sewers, steeply, despite
The tread that goes on ringing like an anvil
Under the striding A. I crook
My arm to shield my face, for we must pass
Beneath the huge, decapitated cross,
White on the wall, the T, and I cannot halt
The tread, the beat of it, it is my own heart,
The walls of my room rise, it is still night,
I have woken again before the word was spelt.

27 September 1946 WKBK, ITGOL, CP

To a Very Slow Air

The golden sheep are feeding, and
Their mouths harbour contentment;
Gladly my tongue praises
This hour scourged of dissension
By weight of their joyous fleeces.

The cloven hills are kneeling,
The sun such an anointment
Upon the forehead, on the hands and feet,
That all air is appointed
Our candid clothing, our elapsing state.

29 September 1946 WKBK, TS, ITGOL, CP

[304]

'At the chiming of light upon sleep'

At the chiming of light upon sleep
A picture relapsed into the deep
Tarn, the hardly-stirring spring
Where memory changes to prefiguring.
Was it myself walking across that grass?
Was it myself, in a rank Michaelmas,
Closed among laurels? It was a green world,
Unchanging holly with the curled
Points, cypress and conifers,
All that through the winter bears
Coarsened fertility against the frost.
Nothing in such a sanctuary could be lost.
And yet, there were no flowers.

                  Morning, and more
Than morning, crosses the floor.
Have I been wrong, to think the breath
That sharpens life is life itself, not death?
Never to see, if death were killed,
No desperation, perpetually unfulfilled,
Would ever go fracturing down in ecstasy?
Death quarrels, and shakes the tree,
And fears are flowers, and flowers are generation,
And the founding, foundering, beast-instructed mansion
Of love called into being by this same death
Hangs everywhere its light. Unsheath
The life you carry and die, cries the cock
On the crest of the sun: unlock
The words and seeds that drove
Adam out of his undeciduous grove.

4 October 1946 WKBK, ITGOL, CP

[305]

'Many famous feet have trod'

Many famous feet have trod
Sublunary paths, and famous hands have weighed
The strength they have against the strength they need;
And famous lips interrogated God
Concerning franchise in eternity;
And in many differing times and places
Truth was attained (a moment's harmony);
Yet endless mornings break on endless faces:

Gold surf of the sun, each day
Exhausted through the world, gathers and whips
Irrevocably from eclipse;
The trodden way becomes the untrodden way,
We are born each morning, shelled upon
A sheet of light that paves
The palaces of sight, and brings again
The river shining through the field of graves.

Such renewal argues down
Our unsuccessful legacies of thought,
Annals of men who fought
Untiringly to change their hearts to stone,
Or to a wafer's poverty,
Or to a flower, but never tried to learn
The difficult triple sanity
Of being wafer, stone, and flower in turn.

Turn out your pockets on the tablecloth:
Consider what we know. A silver piece:
That's life; and, dealing in dichotomies,
This old discoloured copper coin is death.
Turn it about: it is impenetrable.
Reverse and observe, neither bear
A sign or word remotely legible:
But spin the silver to a sphere,

Look in, and testify. Our mortal state
In turn is twisted in a double warp:
The light is waking and the dark is sleep
And twice a day before their gate
We kneel between them. There is more
Knowledge of sleep than death, and yet
Who knows the nature of our casting there,
Trawled inaccessible pool, or set

A line to haul its logic into speech?
Easier to balance on the hand
The waking that our senses can command,
For jewels are pebbles on a beach
Before this weaving, scattering, winged-and-footed
Privilege, this first, untold
And unrecurring luck that is never completed
Even in distance out of our hands' hold,

That makes, this waking traffic, this one last,
One paramount division. I declare
Two lineages electrify the air,
That will like pennons from a mast
Fly over sleep and life and death
Till sun is powerless to decoy
A single seed above the earth:
Lineage of sorrow: lineage of joy;

No longer think them aspects of the same;
Beyond each figured shield I trace
A different ancestry, a different face,
And sorrow must be held to blame
Because I follow it to my own heart
To find it feeding there on all that's bad:
It is sanctionable and right
Always to be ashamed of being sad.

Ashamed that sorrow's beckoned in
By each foiled weakness in the almanac
Engendered by the instinct-to-turn-back
– Which, if there are sins, should be called a sin –
Instinct that so worships my own face
It would halt time herewith
And put my wishes in its place:
And for this reason has great fear of death.

Because tides wound it;
The scuttling sand; the noose
Of what I have and shall lose,
Or have not and cannot get;
Partings in time or space
Wound it; it weeps sorely;
Holds sorrow before its face,
And all to pretend it is not part of me,

The blind part. I know what it will not know:
All stopping-up of cracks
Against dissolution builds a house of wax,
While years in wingspans go
Across and over our heads. Watch them:
They are flying east. They are flying to the ebb
Of dark. They are making sorrow seem
A spider busy on a forgotten web.

They are calling every fibre of the world
Into rejoicing, a mile-long silken cloth
Of wings moving lightwards out of death:
Lineage of joy into mortality hurled,
Endowing every actual bone
With motionless excitement. If quick feet
Must tread sublunary paths, attest this one:
Perpetual study to defeat

Each slovenly grief; the patience to expose
Untrue desire; assurance that, in sum,
Nothing's to reach, but something's to become,
That must be pitched upon the luminous,
Denying rest. Joy has no cause:
Though cut to pieces with a knife,
Cannot keep silence. What else should magnetize
Our drudging, hypocritical, ecstatic life?

15 October 1946 WKBK, ITGOL, CP

Blues Shouter

There ain't no music
East side of this city
That's mellow like mine is,
That's mellow like mine.

Wooden guitar, light cavern
Where the strings pound:
Hideout, haven,
Romping walk of sound.

Innocent beat
No one can imprison,
No one can rob or cheat,
Bully or argue down.

Honour the shaking
Chamber under a hand:
Untouchable, talking,
Coherent diamond.

Here making a heaven –
Hive of sound,
Of joy, driven
All wild and underground.

8 November 1946 WKBK

'That girl is lame: look at my rough'

That girl is lame: look at my rough
Hands. Can there be skill enough
On earth to ease the bone back to its place?
Is human patience wise enough to trace
Wandering pain? And were I allowed to find
Grief's mainspring, could as sick a mind
Give comfort?

               Among such roots to intercede
What flawless fingers I should need,
Hands I have not, hands I could only gain
By an apprenticeship so free from pain
All would have been made new. But at that spring,
She would not look to me for anything.

13 December 1946 WKBK, TS

'Voices round a light'

Voices round a light
Search through the cold,
From house to house
Carrying precious news
Of feet, that on this night
Leave prints of gold.

Hour by hour their breath
Dissolves against the frost
That they deny with singing;
A climbing ladder of song
From barns of death
Against the ungentle stars is gently lost.

Now hands hold up the light
They are so certain of,
That lays their faith
On darkness like a wreath,
A crowning. Voices that melt the night,
Unfearing voices, can you have strength enough?

17 December 1946 WKBK, TS

Thaw

Tiny immortal streams are on the move:
The sun his hand uncloses like a statue,
Irrevocably: thereby such light is freed
That all the dingy hospital of snow
Dies back to ditches. Chalkbeds of heaven bear
These nameless tributaries, but they run
To earth. For here their pouring river reigns;
Here, busy with resurrection, sovereign waters
Confer among the roots, causing to fall
From patient memory forestfuls of grief.

How easily it falls, how easily I let drift
On the surface of morning feathers of self-reproach:
How easily I disperse the scolding of snow.

December? 1946 WKBK, ITGOL, CP

VERSE DRAMAS

BEHIND THE FACADE
or
'Points of View'

A Masque intended for performance
on Midsummer's Eve in Winifred Avenue.
All characters are non-existent.

Prologue

Chorus: It is evening, and the machine is running under its
   own power.
 The ribbon roads have been warmed all day by the sun
 And the hot rubber feet of those who hum along them,
 On this longest midsummer day.
 Now the bank-clerk, the fitter, the body-painter sally forth
 In endless sexual procession along the ever-moving
   pavement
 To dare life to a combat. Some go to tennis clubs
 Where they grip bound racquets, hear the spang of balls
   across gut all around them;
 Some go to littered common and lie, alone or embracing,
   under the exquisite sapphire sky
 Crushing cigarette-ends in bracken roots, boots in ferns;
 Some straddle motor-bikes, goggling at A.A. signs
 Or read fingered books from a branch library.
 The great chants of the churches of mass-production ceased,
   the song of the living
 Is taken up by numberless particles and constituents, and is
   carried to the city's corners,
 Rejoicing in doorways under unlit streetlamps, forgetful of
   crouching Diesel or endless belt.
 Alone and singing, let the people wander, awaiting the
   moon,
 Sniffing the fumed air, realising mysteries,
 Gaining free the magical moods of alcohol.

(The Curtain slowly rises.)

(Winifred Avenue is the scene. The stage shows a cross-section of it, as seen from the shut-in end. Houses stretch away down each side of the stage, showing a bend to the right, going downhill. The houses are all facades – merely and obviously stage-cloth propped up on a frame – but all the hedges in the front gardens are neatly trimmed and the lawns well mown. They are called 'The Hollies'; 'Holmdale'; 'The Elms'; 'West View'; 'The Laurels'; 'Mon Abri'; &c., &c.)

Chorus: When the wind wafts, Winifred Avenue hears not
  nor feels:
Tight-mortared brick rooms, armchair-packed,
No knee space, form simple dormitories
For the man who rises at the alarm's shriek,
Shaves, and munches milky cereal
Before crawling to work in a mass-produced car.
The rabble of traffic leaves her unmoved:
Nothing breaks the stillness of her afternoons
But the rattle of a lawn-mower over grass,
The cries of boys, clambering in apple-trees,
Or the murmur of scales.
Evening brings, not relaxation, but a change of work;
And its inhabitants go out to gaze at shadows shown in
  shadowy marble palaces,
Or to dash between hedges, consuming petrol,
Fleeing from the immortal soul, radio full on.
But hark! the law approaches. O give ear.

(Policeman walks slowly up on right hand side of the street from back stage, pauses on pavement, then crosses the road, pausing halfway to sing.)

Policeman: Nothing ever happens here;
  But then, that's not very queer;
  Balls bounce into roads, children chasing, a swerve
  Tests all the brakes and upbraces the nerve

– And that's all it does its great country to serve
Nothing ever happens here.

Chorus: Nothing, nothing, nothing, nothing,
Nothing ever happens here.

Polcmn: A burglar once was reported
But even then I was thwarted;
A window agape at the back of a house
Proved to be caused by a maid with a grouse
And the safe-cracking sound, we suppose, was a mouse–
Nothing ever happens here.

Chorus: Nothing, nothing, nothing, nothing,
Nothing ever happens here.

(*Policeman continues majestic way across road, and commences to walk down the left hand pavement. He pauses, however, to speak to Mr Smith, who strolls from his house and leans on his gate.*)

Mr Smith: A mild night, Constable.

Polcmn: Very pleasant, Mr Smith, I'm sure. Still, it's about time we had some summer, isn't it?

Mr Smith: It is, indeed. The crops need all the sun they can get now, don't they?

Polcmn: That's right, sir, they do. Wife keeping well?

Mr Smith: Oh yes, quite well, thank you, Constable. She's-er-a little worried by the international situation, I think. I suppose we all are.

Polcmn (expansively):   There ain't nothing to worry about. All newspaper talk. Nothing ever happens. Well, I must be getting along.

Mr Smith: I trust you're right, Constable. Goodnight.

Polcmn: Goodnight, sir. (*Slowly exit*)

[319]

(Mr Smith continues to lean on his gate, staring at the sky pensively. Slowly he takes out his pipe, but puts it back again.)

Semi-chorus I:
What is borne
breeze torn
along the streets
What song to the heart beats
Slow grows
in the rose
light of the
utterly
perfect evening?

Semi-chorus II:
Memories
hop like fleas
out of their
downstair
dwellings. December
recalled in September;
lingering fragrance
of August vagrance
dust-kicking, knapsack
on straight back;
or warm sand
trickling over hand.

Mr Smith: The printed evening columns tell
Of double century, as well
As uprisings, air-consuming records,
White-shorted athletes snatching seconds
From previous figures. By guileful tricks
Someone took eight for twenty-six,
But ghosts of murmuring sunlit grounds
Flicker away when presses pound.
Theirs is the summer: I, alas,

Seem to have allowed it to pass,
And can only myself recapture
Through other's rapture.
One wonders, really, whether there has been
All the fun I am told I have seen . . .
Slipped, Like a clinging climber,
And silence.

Chorus: What is abroad, this summer night?
There is a calmness in the air
Unfolding hearts are unaware.
Soul, up-mounting like a kite,
Still is held by earthly chain;
But illusive unreality
Induces sentimentality
Memories surge again
Like the last hymn
Breaking sun-lit across the school
Impatient of rule
The term grown dim.

Mr Smith: Where is the Smith who, calling frantically,
Burst defences, took pass, handed off and scored?
Beneath the tapering posts against the grey sky?
The Smith who steadily and calm defended
His wicket until relief came, play was ended?

Chorus: Gone like a leaf
whirled by the wind
however you seek
you never will find.

Mr Smith: Mourning for one's youth, who can say
Were it again, I could live it no fuller?
Who can claim to have lived every day to the ultimate
    second
Undaunted by Death's yellow finger nails
And long black box?

Chorus: However you seek
  you never will find
  gone with the leaves
  whirled with the wind.

Mr Smith: The shy Smith who sat on the edge of a sofa
  Taking tea, and balancing a plate on his knees,
  Nearly fainting when she spoke to him
  Writing poems with an office pen . . .
  Where is he?

Chorus: You will meet him, soon enough.

Mr Smith: I suppose I must accept the fact
  That these things do not come within the scope
  Of the senior clerk.
  After all, we have water and gas,
  Electricity, and the park . . .
  We must abandon the Cape of Good Hope.

                  (Enter Mrs Smith from Smith's front door.)

Mrs Smith: Dear, have you seen Diana's schoolbag? She's lost
  it again.

Mr Smith: No, dear, not unless it's under the wireless?

Mrs Smith: No, she's looked there. How quiet it is tonight . . .
  I think I shall stay out a little.

Mr Smith: Now I come to think of it, I did see something like
  a schoolbag in the kennel . . . the dog had her pups in it.
  I'll go and see. (*Exit*)

Mrs Smith (leaning on gate):
  So many houses, curtains, front doors, windows,
  So much cleaning, washing, rubbing, polishing,
  Back-breaking labour (luckily borne by a maid)
  So many bridge games, and the illusion of society,
  An office dance in winter, friends in,

Relatives round the fire, coming in Ford V.8's
And leaving a smell of cigarette smoke and sherry.
In the summer we gain high ground and picnic on hill:
And go to see John play for the School second team,
And Diana lose a tennis tournament.
At Christmas and in winter we mount a five-foot billiard
    table in the dining room, and John makes quite large
    breaks and beats his father
And we take bicarbonate.

Chorus: The seasons change –
    None can deny it.
Rearrange
    Them? Just you try it!
Use your ration card
    Don't strike it
Although your meat is hard
    You'd better like it.

Mrs Smith: When I was young
    New songs were sung
    But now I've forgotten the tunes.

Chorus: We all know
    The evening's aglow
    But there's no need to open old wounds.

Mrs Smith: When I was young, the black-laced fat-faced
        singing mistress said to me:
            Learn to dance
            And you'll have a chance
    In any musical comedy.

    Underneath the bedroom, hanging light shook, rattled like a
        skeleton in gibbet chains
            While I was romancing,
            Singing, dancing
    Visualised my name in a thousand Drury Lanes.

[323]

Chorus: Soul, mounting like a balloon
  Opal on a string
  Of sentiment, umbilical to earth.

Mrs Smith: That that happened after that
  I need not mention now;
  The memory of spaded earth
  Beneath a budding bough
  Striking wooden lid
  Struck me, horrid; I wept.
  Penury poked her nose where the radiogram used to
    stand;
  And marriage relieved the family of one element.
  No more rooms at the Grand.

Chorus: Let us sing of south coast boarding houses,
    and the daughters of retired colonels;
  Cobwebbed stables, where the door creaks;
  Spinsters with faces like prunes, and music lessons.
  Let us give moan for the tragedy of unfruited wombs
  And wail for artistic embroidery.
  When the seasons change, and the sea, like a leaping grey
    mastiff,
  Splashes ten yards of the empty promenade
  And the rain, seen through lace curtains, is wetter and more
    icy on the front
  And the aspidestra [*sic*] grows smuggly out of its evil pot.
  Then one knows full horror in the waste of bed-sittingrooms,
    haunted by culinary smells
  Waiting for the sky to stop falling, so that one can post the
    weekly letter to the school friend.

    (Enter Cuthbert Shrive, the bookseller, from the house.)

C.S.: Ah, good evening, Mrs Smith, a beautiful evening, is it
    not?
  Summer is really with us at last.

[324]

Mrs Smith: Quite charming, Mr Shrive. But I'm afraid I must
       go in.
    I have a lot to see to. Goodnight. (*sotto voce*) Ugh!

C.S.:   Goodnight! . . . (*he minces out of his gate. Four members of
    the Chorus, disguised as school captains, take part in the following
    period*)

    Searching – in purely *experimental*
    Capacity, of course – certain Continental
    Publications, one discovers –
    Or should I, haply, say 'reveals'? –
    Print on thoughts, slippery as eels,
    Not only of lovers
    Alluring to me
    And those of my 'kind'
    (vulgar words
    suiting birds)
    Tee-hee! Tee-hee! Tee-hee!

4 S.C.'s: You who cast the first stone
    Remember us:
    For he was once as straight and clean as we.

C.S.:   We whose minds are like coffee stains
    Or bruises in peaches;
    Attracted to little girls in trains
    And boys on beaches
    Looking sideways over our noses
    With clerical laughs
    At the academy of erotic poses
    On photographs.

4 S.C.'s: Into the world, on the wings of wind, he came;
    Bruised, he retreated; now, lame,
    He hobbles down life's back streets
    Denouncing drunkenness and buying children sweets

C.S.:   What delights
   Sweeten our nights
   When alone we writhe in the cold light of the moon!
   We few, we happy few, we band of . . .

Chorus: Buggers!

C.S.:   . . . brothers
   Cut off from the world of others,
   The bank clerk, billiard player, and the buffoon.
   Our souls are wound round and round
       Tight; that nothing can be found:
   Like a rose, or a dirty screwed handkerchief.
   Keeping out light, morals, and purity,
       And with equal obdurity
   The manifestations of a worldly grief.

4 *S.C.'s*:   Hear, O hear the full defence.

C.S.:   I must confess that not always was I of this party;
   If I cared to pause and consider
   I could remember a time when Greece signified more than
       Oscar Wilde;
   At home, if I cared to burrow under old relics, I could find
       books of poems
   Flowers of adolescence, their theme sadness and despair
   And an unhappy love. O, what dreams I had!
   At night, when I looked over the orchard at home, and saw
       round apples, globular in the moonlight
   How full my heart would be of dark peace!
   Then, how I longed to portray English life,
   In one royal surge from golden Runneymede
   In psalms of freedom, and falling palms across the sunlit
       path of our summers!
   Or the seasons – how I tried to harden my thoughts to the
       texture of thick ice, or let them be frost
   As I surveyed the iron clods broken over the fields
   Or the sun intricately patterning the snow;

[326]

How I tried to let myself sink on the scent of hay
Watching the reaper pause to drink as he leant on his scythe
    against the blue sky;
Alas! that has gone. What dreams had I of life and passion
Seeing love as a mating of eagles
A consummation of the two fire-hearted beings
As swift as deer
Tawny like lions;
A voyage, in quest of a casket, blazing with stones.
Then I remember
My love's long and humiliating history
From the time when, as a boy at a prep school, I worshipped
    the younger mistress;
Passing through the usual romantic friendships
Into the buffets of deeper passions on stormier seas;
Always, always, always defeated
Always the loser, always he who bore the lost standard
Left to bury the dead when the armies had departed
And to weep over sunlit mounds.

4 S.C.'s: World, what have you done
    To one who meant no harm?
    Desired to laugh in the sun,
    Sleep, head on arm,
    Through nights of quiet trees
    And silent growth of flowers
    Desired to break the sweeping surf
    In salt-drenched hours.

Chorus: His was not the part of heroism, or the defended
    gate;
    No steel sword held his cause in mailed hand
    No vizor was lifted at the day's close
    To kiss lifted lips.
    He asked of life passion
    And the Grecian heritage
    Wished to live as fully as he felt

Gave body, mind, soul, Trinity united to purpose
Gained reports of Police Courts, plain envelopes, and
    peculiar magazines
With his fortieth year, still unfulfilled, still
    half-hoping, still damned to live.

4 S.C.'s: Now his defence was one of despair
    And of making the best of things
    When there is nothing to make the best of.

C.S.:   Dear me! I had almost forgotten. Ernest promised to
    ring up . . . (*hurries into his house*)

        (School Captains rejoin the Chorus)

Chorus: Midsummer's Eve draws on apace
    But yet more feel the evening's peace in their hearts
    And amble out to see the sun slowly die at last;
    See the alliance of Church and State, leaning on their garden
    fences
    What are their defences?

(From their houses, which are next door to each other, the Rev.
Incent and Mr Cranuloid come. They lean over the dividing fence.)

M.C.:   Beautiful day it's been.

R.I.:   Yes, it has, hasn't it? Quite like summer, really.

M.C.:   This happens to be Midsummer's Eve.

R.I.:   Of course . . . how time does fly! Do you know, when I
    was a boy we should be right in the heart of summer by
    now, and, well, look at the rain we had only yesterday.

M.C. *(reflectively)*:   Yes . . . it's a long time since I was young.

R.I.:   Yes . . . I was brought up at my father's Rectory. I still
    remember those evening services, with the rooks in the
    trees . . . how long ago it all seems!

M.C. (*savagely*):
　　For me there was no Rectory, quiet-bricked behind laurel
　　　　bushes,
　　Or a pasture, clotted with dung, where the horses galloped.
　　I remember, I remember
　　Streets stuck with lamp-posts
　　Boarded windows haunted by ghosts
　　Of those who had come, and passed on
　　To where Money had gone.
　　Father shirt-sleeved, bending
　　Over mother maimed with mending
　　Every week washing was taken in like penance
　　Thee was a gaslit Parish Hall, but no urge to dance
　　Where I came from.
　　From my cradle, even as I would grasp
　　A spoon, as later I hoped my pen would rasp
　　Signing men's executions
　　I wanted to fight society on its own ground
　　With its own weapons, unarmed at the start,
　　To gain hold, and to defeat the ladies in high-powered cars
　　And those who were scratch at fashionable courses.
　　But alas! the odds were too greatly piled
　　To allow more than a modest share in the booty
　　One has to do more than defy to gain Monte Carlo and the
　　　　white villa
　　And so I live here, away from squalor and luxury,
　　Unable to do evil.

Chorus:　We are very grieved to learn
　　　　Of your end;
　　Without money, without evil,
　　　　Without friend:
　　In the waters of finance you took a short hop,
　　When it got deeper, you had to stop;
　　And it seems that you've been what resembles a flop
　　　　For you couldn't lend
　　　　Or ascend.

R.I.:   Hearing your tale of woe, I weep.
   Such reveries as haunt one's sleep
   Are these, but coming not in dreaming
   But in full force, this pearly evening;
   I weep; but blacker recollection tells
   Of intenser purgatories, deeper Hells,
   Calling for utterance.

Chorus: Speak: only the wind will hear.

R.I.:   Small tragedies are Othellos to their actors.
   I, too, swore reverently, over the tree-tops,
   As the world settled to rest behind the elms.
   I remember the fire of the Gospels, flame of grace,
   The whiteness of the Lord, like sacerdotal linen,
   Or Spring cherry-blossom, a-foam on the trees,
   Beauty beyond expression, I devoted all I was ever likely to
      have to the Church.
   Nor did the fire die immediately:
   The white fire of devotion was transmuted into social
      progress, and a living was gained
   Where one mentioned souls as frequently as legs
   And received same glances when one did.
   At first, a little of the power remained;
   What I had, I lost; I have gained nothing but shame and a
      false position,
   Done nothing but organised teas, handed round cups,
   Preached on Sundays, and frowned at the whispering choir;
   Debarred from the needful class by fear and convention,
   Betrayer of the cause I privately swore to uphold,
   Mincing about the congregation, impotent to inspire,
   Cackling about Crucifixion, and quailing at gossip,
   Weeping without feeling, praying without thinking,
   Offering without humility, praising when blaming,
   Taking without giving, dying without duty.
   (*enraged, tears off collar*)
         I feel an urge

To burn this scourge,
This social catch!

M.C.: Allow me to lend you a match of my misery.
(*hands match; R.I. ceremoniously burns collar, and drops it*)

Chorus: Now a symbol has been enacted, the actors stare,
   feeling a little foolish,
 Conscious of having made a gesture at the whirling stars.
 But reality whips –

R.I.: Caught in the morass, we can still see the stars!
    That is the tragedy.
 Still to know the essential horror of this avenue . . .
 This avenue! This cursed blockend avenue!

(*Enter Mrs Smith*)

M.C.: Detonated dynamite
 Might destroy it.

(*Enter Mr Smith*)

Mrs S.: What mortal methods can kill the canker?

(*Enter Mr Shrive*)

Mr S.: Eaten opium
 Might alloy it.

C.S.: But when our souls are held at anchor?

Chorus: Paon rising, resonant, revolution, re-echoing . . .

All: Drag down the facade, and show what lies behind it!
 The visiting agony of a routine mind
 Caught unawares in the still of summer!
 Change our lot, our day, our avenue;
 Make every newcomer to the city sue to see it first!
 Fame for the facade: fulfill our worldly want!
 Let us destroy Winifred Avenue with postcards and brass
   toasting-forks;

Force cars to crawl up its narrowness, or humbly kneel at the
    bottom,
Putting sixpences at toll-gates, to see the sights.

Chorus: You cannot do it;
   You are too old.

All: Let us see journalists, pen-licking, leaning on our gates
   Demanding private interviews from behind the facade
   As from a zoo. We must have tea-rooms, and here
   A fountain.

Chorus: Years slipped, more waiting, eating, sliding
   You cannot do it.

All: Where there's a will there's a way,
   Faint heart never won the day.

Chorus: Cease winning conflict with clichés
   You cannot do it.

All: Let him stand forth who says we cannot!

Chorus: In your hearts the traitors stand
   Knowing;
   Defeating you at poker hands
   Not showing.
   When triumphant voices deny losing
   There are voices true, accusing,
   Secretly the facts are oozing
   Conviction is growing.

All: If we cannot, where is he who will?
   Where is he who will sign our name in flame-letters on the
     clouds
   And put three-inch headlines in the daily papers?
   Whose mouth is kissed in the South,
   Who is feasted in the East
   Caressed in the West
   And cheered in the North – let him stand forth.

Deliver us! Raise us from our topiaried tomb!
Stanley!
Stanley of thirty-eight! He shall bear the torch to our dark
    places, make our souls like snowy peaks
Thrusting at the blue sky!

Chorus: He is leaving, he is going away.

All: Let him take to the world the essence of our sorrow
    He must not be ignorant of the ways of life
    Or Winifred's horror. Turn his heart against brick, and
       clipped hedges,
    Let him rend suburbia apart with a blow from his bronzed
       hand
    And lead our ranks away from cheap radiograms
    And stuffed armchair comfort. (*Stanley appears at window*)
    You must keep your eyes fixed on the frosty stars
    And your feet must ring on the metallic road.
    Save us, we cry; you are our hope.
    Bear our tribulations with you, and remember their bitterness
    As you indulge in guerilla warfare with unpaid bills
    Or tramp the golf-course with a business friend,
    And when the hand points the hour, strike, and let our
       chains fall like feathers
    And let us know the world again, of the tiger and the year's
       spring.
    Approach.

       (*Stanley descends from window and appears at door*)

Stanley: Because I am going beyond sea
    You ask something of me
    Which I do not understand.

All: Look around you, look around you, at the genteel slates
    The numbered houses, and the painted gates
    At the routine that saddles us, and wearies our souls
    And reminds us of our fall from grace.

Stanley: All have I known, directly, or indirectly.

All: We beg deliverance from them, and a state of freedom
   – Either by fame, or revolution.
   Winifred has our hate
   Our blackest hate.

Stanley: Yet I do not understand
   When the flickering candle shows deeper wrinkles
   And hand gropes for chairback, pathetic,
   I shall remember the faded garland.
   I shall remember the sunlit hours gliding across the ground
   Lengthening with the shadows of fielders;
   The shut of desk will bring memories
   Of ink-smells, of books lost and found;
   Sung hymns will return at a struck note
   Bringing unavoidable associations.
   I shall remember the yearly migrations
   Taking the south coast by rote:
   Hastings, Eastbourne, and Bournemouth twice,
   Teignmouth and Falmouth,
   Then Newquay, Ilfracombe and Weston-Super-Mare
   All beaten out under the railway wheels to paradise;
   To a memory, a few rapidly ageing photographs,
   And perhaps a wooden spade chopped up for firewood in
      the cold winter;
   The recollection of golden beachdays
   And gently riding rafts.
   But most of all I shall remember home
   However guised, in what dress, design, of kind;
   I shall remember
   The billiard table and th'instructive tome,
   The giddy heights of stairs, and kitchen shapes,
   Furtive glances into sisters' room,
   Early sun through window, crumbs and magazine in bed,
   Uncle's humour and the Christmas grapes.
   I shall remember frost binding back-garden loam,

The silent trees in the snow,
The slippery doorstep, the dead sky,
And Spring breaking across winter like foam,
The rising sap, new leaves, and blossom, white,
Dew on the grass, and cutting winds in March.
Then summer and the cindered heat; hot brick,
Noon sun making hall appear like night
To eyes fresh from hot dust and the cries of friends;
Languorous afternoons in crab-like appletrees
Freckled green and gold; the peacefulness
That nearby shunting to the evening lends
When the lone star hangs in the turquoise skies
Outside the bedroom window,
When the springs seem soft as angel's wings to tired
    body,
And memory slips away with sleep, and late birds' cries.
And these will return to me, and I shall remember my youth
    like an old song
When I have time to glance to the shore from the waves, for
    a second.

(*During his speech the householders have gradually dispersed to
their houses, and are now leaning on their gates, displaying none
of the enthusiam they seemed to feel earlier.*)

Chorus: You take our advice
   If life isn't nice
   The fault's with you
   Points of view
   Reveal that some
   Are happy, handsome,
   Rich, or carefree;
   You're contrary,
   You are a misfit
   All along
   Though you don't think it
   You are wrong.

Stanley (picking his suitcase up, which has a large label reading 'World' on it):
And so now the time has come to take leave of you.
Do not think that I shall forget, in the vortex of faces
You and your ways;
Unconsciously, you will be my touchstone,
Until death. *(To Mr Smith)* Goodbye.

Mr Smith: May your memory bring nothing but pleasure.

Stanley (to Mrs Smith):   Goodbye.

Mrs Smith: May every hour be spent well.

Stanley (to Mr Shrive):   Goodbye.

C.S.:   May your hair stay golden.

Stanley (to Rev. Incent and Mr Cranuloid):   Goodbye.

R.I. and M.C.:   May you succeed, carelessly free,
Not consciously fail, as we.

Stanley (to all):   Goodbye.

All: Godspeed we wish you to the world,
Happiness till flag be furled
And wings curled:
May the day bring you delight
Sleep come with night
And oblivion quite.

(Stanley leaves the stage. The others wave after him until they lose sight of him. Unnoticed, a street lamp has come on, and the collar is lying beneath it. The householders slowly and pensively return to their houses, and the light of day fades. At last the sole lighting is that of the street lamp, with the collar in the pool of light it casts.)

Chorus: And so we have taken him away
From the sunlit land where moon-daisies sway

In green fields;
What will he do, how will he bear his scars?
O, it no longer depends on the stars
What he yields.

But he will never come back.
For his feet are firmly set on the oneway track
Of life;
Others will laugh in his place:
He has taken the prize for his success in the race
And is meeting the strife.

[*September–October 1939*] TS

Night in the plague

(A city house. Tall window curtains. Entrance to hall and street door and a stair rising along the back of the stage. Baggage piled near hall entrance. Sparse furnishing suggesting removal. Clock on wall. Bell pull. Anne is sitting with sewing in her lap but reading a letter. This she hastily puts away at the entrance of her father. He is a small and elderly dapper decisive man.)

(Time. Late evening: summer.)

Father   I would not have left you in a servantless house
    So long, but upon business. There was much to be done,
    Much to be decided. This is worse than a war.
    A battle or two on foreign ground is nothing,
    It clears the streets of quarrelsome boys and beggars:
    Trade can be kept up. This is a different case.
    No ships come up the river, the customs are idle:
    Our cargoes cannot be taken; nothing received,
    Nothing unloaded. Those workmen who are not sick
    We have turned away. I have just closed the office,
    And our clerks, that pick their teeth with their pens,
    Can idle somewhere else.
                    One today
    Was taken with the sickness.

Anne   Did he know it?

Father   Yes.
    He was looking over a bill for the sixth time,
    Wasting an hour for want of proper work.
    Then he complained of the heat, and pulled his collar,
    Called for brandy and a wet pad for his head.
    Later he vomited. I sent him home,
    And watched his feet go in and out of the gutter,
    Already lost to him.

Anne   What was his name?

Father   Heatherton. His father put him at my charge
  Nine months back. He would never have made a merchant.
  (*drinking a glass of wine*) And this to clear
  The sourness of the weather.

Anne   I have heard
  Hardly a sound from the street all day.
  Never a crying of goods, or noise of wheels,
  Or management of horses, or neighbours' talk.
  Is the city quiet?

Father   Empty, as if something were passing near,
  All'd gone to gape at. There's a deal of muttering:
  Such a one is absent: he's dead or kept in his house,
  Or is gone to the country; the bills of dead were so many:
  The Lord Mayor and Sheriffs now deliberate
  A curfew; such a number were buried
  In a great pit at Cripplegate – O, there's no end to it.
  All Bedlam's loose. There's one goes wailing about
  In rags – 'Lord, pity us! Lord, have mercy upon us!'
  I whacked him with my stick to clear the road.
  Is supper ready?

Anne   All on the table:
  Mainly cold scraps.

Father   Sufficient for now. Throw away the leavings.
  An empty house breeds rats,
  And from tomorrow this will be empty enough.
  All valuable things like plate and candlesticks
  I have put in the bank's keeping, likewise my money
  And papers of business, barring a sum
  For the journey and our care at my brother's house.
  Lucky that money does not catch the sickness!

Anne   What time do we start?

Father   Between four and five in the morning.
  You'll need sleep lighter than a tipped scale, Anne,

To wake in readiness. But I will call you.
The odds are that I shall not go to bed,
But sit accounting. Time enough for sleep
In the country, intolerable time.

Anne Father:
There's something I want to ask you that will not wait,
Not even till morning.

Father Say it, then.

Anne It concerns James Ekall –
That will displease you.

Father Does he want to marry you again?
Well. I forbad him once. I'll forbid him twice.
Take him that answer.

Anne No. It's nothing of that.
I know your wishes, and I know my own,
And yours must be obeyed. It is this only:
I know you think it death to stay in London.

Father More likely than not.

Anne He lives alone, as if in his own mind,
Lives carelessly, seems not to care
Whether he lives at all. The playhouses are shut,
There's nothing for him to do. I feel
If I leave now with you, and he stays here,
He'll die without my seeing him again.

Father Many will have to stay.

Anne I know.
Pity for one should rightly be for all.
But I am weak and pity only one!
Father, I ask it of your charity:
Take him with us.

Father With us!
You ask too much.

Anne   Not all the way, not even half the way:
  Get him out of the city. If at this time
  You had a nephew, or a poorer cousin,
  Or an old friend's son in your care, would you think twice
  Before you took him out of harm? To me
  He's more than friend or cousin. But if you will,
  Don't think of that. Think of him as one
  You have power to help.

Father   But I could help anyone,
  Men I have known for years – Macy, Alardyce,
  Prentice, their wives, or their families –
  Even my own clerks would go if they could.

Anne   If they are your choice, take them.
  But since it's dangerous to stay,
  Take someone; and since you can only take one,
  Take James: because of all outside my duty
  I wish him safe.

Father   Has he put you to this?

Anne   No, he has not.

Father   Why cannot he help himself?
  The roads are not shut, he is not penniless.
  He has two legs. There is nothing to keep him here,
  No business or ties of family.
  The city is not besieged.

Anne   All true, and so I have told him.
  He would not go while I was here; and now
  I am afraid he will linger, and be despairing,
  And make no shift for himself. He may learn
  Of the death of one he knows, or see
  Red crosses on doors, or hear the death cart creak,
  And say, tomorrow I will move, or else next week,
  And be considering whether he move or not,
  And come across a book that argues it

Four ways – and all the time
The pestilence moves on him, and he is caught,
And all's past argument.

Father   Will he not go because you wish it?

Anne   He has written me a letter
Saying, in sum, he thinks I keep his heart,
And what of him is fit to be preserved
I carry from harm.

Father   Last time we met, I told him he was a fool,
And so he is. Say I do what you ask:
When are we rid of him? They are shutting their doors,
In the country, to London people; wisely, too.
Are we to set him in the road
Between here and Gloucester? Leave him to peck for food
Like a hen? No, it will be my care
To find some place where he can go on mooning,
My money and name will have to buy him safety.

Anne   He'll pay you back.

Father   Yes, if he doesn't forget, or find a book
Arguing that he shouldn't. Anne,
I would do much for you, because you are
My only child; between us is love, not duty.
But this request seems all unreasonable.
If he himself had asked me, say to be carried
To a certain spot, where he has friends – or if
He had given me money to find him board at Gloucester –
But am I to lug him from his bed unasked
At five in the morning? Take him on my back
As my responsibility? Not to be thought of!

Anne   I am thinking of when he will be dead
And we are telling ourselves it's not our fault.

Father   You put too much in my words:
To stay does not mean to die. Many are staying:

[342]

Some have to, for their business requires it,
And they are not thinking themselves as dead;
Others decide by pricking on a text,
And choose by that – If it were death to stay
They'd go without haggling. I tell you, Anne,
By care, clean habits, keeping out of crowds
And poorer streets – and, of course, trust in God –
Many will come unscathed out of this year.
But since you fret so, make to James this offer,
Let him request me formally in a letter
To find him country lodging, and I will do it.
Lord knows I shall have nothing else to do!
Now I will change my clothes, and then to supper.
The air seems greasy as a kitchen.

(Father goes out. Anne hurriedly writes a letter, folds it. Then moves about the room, humming a tune, which develops into a song, to single chords off.)

Love through solitary days
Falls like corn beneath the rain
I am forgetting all your ways –
    When will you come again?
    When will you come again?

Tear away the stone and slating
And the house will not remain,
Take from love the easy meeting
    It will not come again:
    It will not come again.

(James enters either at or towards the end of this song, from the street door entrance.)

James   That's the prettiest noise I have heard in town tonight,
And I have heard some, I can tell you.

Anne   I thought the house was empty.
James, how did you get in? Is anything wrong?

James   I got in through the street door, which was open.
Nothing's more wrong than usual.

Anne   It shouldn't have been open.

James   Perhaps it knew I was coming.
Inanimate things may sometimes be kind to us
Since they're so often cruel. It's no matter.

Anne   The danger of the streets for you!

James   Danger's in everything, they tell me:
In the rim of a cup, in the hangings of a room,
And yet I've heard one attends
Childbeds of pestilence-stricken women
And gets drunk with the money.

Anne   What made you come?

James   I sealed in my letter all
A letter can say, but that's not much.
I had to come and speak the rest myself,
And neither is that much now. Anne, understand
What I have not written or said.

Anne   I had written to you, too, James:
For certain the plague is worsening
Or my father would not go. Listen:
I want you to come with us: we are leaving in the morning.
I have half-talked my father into it; see him, ask
Graciously, and he'll agree. Can you leave so quickly?

James   Go with you? What sort of charity is this?

Anne   Do men think of nothing but money? Here I have told
My father to give you room in the coach – not as he would,
By drawing up a deed with witnesses –
But as one man helping another from danger; now
Must I instruct you how to receive help?

James   Not if it's given willingly. But is it?
My dear, there will be a time when we shall ride

Behind horses in the morning, but we shall be alone,
And go among strangers and strange places;
That day I pray for. But I'm less eager
To travel like a flunkey with your father
As 'Mr James, the young man scared of the plague
Who couldn't be parted from Anne. He's been once
   refused,
But still hangs on like a dog at a fair.'
You know your father's no great love of me.

Anne   I know one thing: the plague can kill, in a day,
Kill you or anyone. Are you blind?
Do you wear magic shirts? What's all
The imagined insult in the world
If death is missed? Where's the morning
We travel to you spoke of, if next week
You're in a pit with twenty more dead men?
– I should not speak so: I am making you angry:
But I am angry when you set
Irrelevant things before our love, knowing
If I had leave to run behind the coach
I'd take it, in your place.

James   Well, since you say so, I will ask to go,
But I would sooner be taking you away
Than being tolerated as your friend.

(Father enters at head of stairs. He is white and dishevelled,
gripping banisters.)

Father   Take her away. Both of you get away.
Out of this house. Forget the coach and the luggage,
Go on foot – she is your care, James.
Is it night still? I fell while dressing,
Then to a faint, and a sick dizziness,
Lasting I know not how long – come to myself,
I searched my body, and found
The plaguespot here on my thigh.

Anne   The plague!

Father   Keep off these stairs!
　I have forgotten when I kissed you last,
　But it was the last. Get your things and go.
　Then I will lock the door and care for myself
　As long as I can.

James   Send for a doctor.　　　　　　　　　　　　*(pulls bellrope)*

Anne   There's no one in the house.

(Death appears behind Father. The clock stops ticking.)

Death   I am in the house.

(A moment of realisation. Father, under the look of Death, goes slowly and unsteadily back into his bedroom. James and Anne at the foot of the stairs.)

　Do not hurry away.
　I offer you safe conduct for tonight.
　Come up these stairs, and see how a man dies.

(James and Anne begin to climb the stairs. The curtain is lowered to denote the passing of a few hours.)

between 15 October and 8 November 1946 WKBK

[346]

APPENDICES

APPENDIX 1
Contents of Collections

(1) Contents of typed booklets prepared by Larkin

The Happiest Day (Summer 1939)

This collection is no longer extant. It was probably destroyed by Larkin, though some poems were saved by him in an early narrative of his writing. These were:

'The sun was battling to close our eyes'
Butterflies: 'Side-stepping, fluttering, quick-flecking'
What the half-opened door said to the empty room 'Waft, waft, thou Summer wind'
A meeting – et seq.: 'Together we stood'
Founder's Day, 1939: (1) 'I looked for a pearl'
                       (2) 'All day the clouds hung over the cathedral'
The days of thy youth: 'Ah, the rock is crumbling'
Plus some 'Collected Fragments'.

Poems in War (3 September–7 October 1939)

This collection is no longer extant. It was probably destroyed by Larkin, though some poems were saved by him in the early narrative of his writing. It included the Masque, *Behind the Facade*. It is numbered 'XV', indicating, possibly, that there were fourteen other poems in *Poems in War*.

One O'Clock Jump (October 1939)

This collection is no longer extant. It was probably destroyed by Larkin; though the file in which it was contained with the cover showing title and date still exists. Some of the poems were saved by Larkin in the narrative of his writing.

Larkin presents the following poems as having been in *Poems in War* or *One O'Clock Jump*:

À un ami qui aime: 'Disparaging my taste in ties'

'The grinding halt of plant, and clicking stiles'
'Smash all the mirrors in your home'
'Watch, my dear, the darkness now'
'Turning from obscene verses to the stars' (VOH)
To James Hogg, 1770–1835: 'Lock the door, Lariston, lock it, I say to
    you' (VOH)
'Has all History rolled to bring us here?'
'In a second I knew: it was your voice speaking'
A study in light and dark: 'The glow, back over the common, comes
    from the railway'
Autumn refrain: 'Autumn sees the sun low in the sky' (VOH)
'Within, a voice said: Cry!'
'What is the difference between December and January?'
'Falling of these early flowers' (VOH)
To a friend's acquaintance: 'Are you innocent? I expect you are'
To a friend: 'O let the passing moon delight'
A farewell: 'Take your tomorrow: go, I give you leave'
Young woman blues: 'So if you saw him not alone'
'Lie there, my tumbled thoughts'
'Now the shadows that fall from the hills'
'The pistol now again is raised'
A song of praise: 'Praise to the higher organisms' (VOH)
Homage to Daddy Lamartine: 'The hills in their recumbent
    postures'

[Ist Collection] (Late 1939) [Untitled]

Untitled sonnet
'Having grown up in shade of Church and State'
The Days of thy Youth: 'Ah, the rock is crumbling'
The Ships at Mylae: 'You are not happy here. Not here'
Alvis Victrix: 'What is this voluptuous monster, painted
    red'
Stanley en Musique: 'The dull whole of the drawing room'
Stanley et la Glace: 'Three pennies gain a twisted whorl'
Erotic Play: 'Your summer will sing for this'

The Village of the Heart (April 1940 [March 28 1940]) 12 poems
by Philip Larkin

Prologue: 'Such is our springtime, sprawling its sprouting'
'Standing on love's farther shores'

'The hills in their recumbent postures'
'Falling of these early flowers'
'So you have been, despite parental ban'
'Through darkness of sowing'
'Praise to the higher organisms'
'Prince, fortune is accepted among these rooms'
'Lock the door, Lariston, lock it, I say to you'
'Nothing significant was really said'
'Turning from these obscene verses to the stars'
'Autumn sees the sun low in the sky'
'The cycles hiss on the road away from the factory'
Epilogue: 'Will hoped-for rains'

Further Poems (July 1940)
    Nine poems of depression

[As Epigraph] 'For who will deny'
After Dinner Remarks: 'A good meal can somewhat repair'
Two Sonnets
    I: The conscript: 'So he evolved a saving fiction as'
    II: The conscientious objector: 'This was the first fruit of his
        resolve'
Further after dinner remarks (extempore): 'I never was much of a
    one for beauty'
Poem: 'Still beauty'
Remark: 'Seconds of tangled love and art'
Sonnet: 'But we must build our walls, for what we are'
Historical Fact: 'Shelley/had a belly'
Midsummer Night 1940: 'The sun falls behind Wales: the town and
    hills'
'But as to the real truth, who knows? The earth'

Poems August 1940

'Art is not clever'
'Unexpectedly the scene attained'
Address to Life, by a Young Man Seeking a Career: 'Freckling
    summers have crossed my brow'
'O today is everywhere'
'There are moments like music, minutes'
Creative Joy: 'Anything or nothing'

'As a war in years of peace'
'As a war in years of peace' (revised version)
'Could wish to lose hands'
'The spaniel on the tennis court'
Schoolmaster
'He sighed with relief, he had got the job. He was safe'
'When we broke up, I walked alone'
'From the window at sundown'
'You've only one life and you'd better not lose it'
'The question of poetry, of course,'
Chorus from a Masque: 'You took our advice'
Rupert Brooke: 'Give him his due – some liked his poetry'
Postscript – On Imitating Auden: 'Imitating you is fairly easy'

Chosen Poems (April 1941)

'The sun was battling to close our eyes'
'This is one of those whiteghosted mornings'
'We see the spring breaking across rough stone'
'Having grown up in shade of Church and State' (from Ist
    Collection)
'Autumn has caught us in our summer wear'
'Why did I dream of you last night?'
'Chorus from a Masque: 'You took our advice' (from Poems[?]
    August 1940)
'When night puts twenty veils'
'Through darkness of sowing' (from The Village of the
    Heart)
'So you have been, despite parental ban' (from The Village of the
    Heart)
'Nothing significant was really said' (from The Village of the Heart)
'Prince, fortune is accepted among these rooms' (from The Village
    of the Heart)
'The hills in their recumbent postures' (from The Village of the
    Heart)
Epilogue: 'Will hoped-for rains' (from The Village of the Heart)
After-Dinner Remarks: 'A good meal can somewhat repair' (from
    Further Poems)
Midsummer Night, 1940: 'The sun falls behind Wales; the towns
    and hills' (from Further Poems)

Two Versions:
  (i) 'Unexpectedly the scene attained' (from Poems[?] August 1940)
  (ii) 'At once he realised that the thrilling night'
'Art is not clever' (from Poems[?] August 1940)
'There are moments like music, minutes' (from Poems[?] August 1940)
'Could wish to lose hands' (from Poems[?] August 1940)
'From windows at sundown' (from Poems[?] August 1940)
'Guests are numerous; for the far arid strand'
'Evening, and I, were young'
'Stranger, do not linger'
The Poet's Last Poem: 'Several eagles crossed my page'
'As a war in years of peace' (from Poems[?] August 1940)
Schoolmaster: 'He sighed with relief. He had got the job. He was safe.' (from Poems[?] August 1940)
'There is no language of destruction for'
Two Preliminary Sonnets:
  (i) 'The world in its flowing is various; as tides'
  (ii) 'But we must build our walls, for what we are'
  ((ii) from Further Poems)
'Out in the lane I pause: the night'
New Year Poem: 'The short afternoon ends; and the year is over'
'Tired of a landscape known too well when young'
' "Interesting, but futile," said his diary'
'Time and Space were only their disguises'
'The house on the edge of the serious wood'

SEVEN POEMS (January 1942)

'A week ago today'
'There behind the intricate carving'
'The Ego's county he inherited' (in *TNS* 'Conscript')
'After the casual growing up'
'Sailors brought back strange stories of those birds'
Dances in Doggerel
  (i) 'How can the sunlight entertain'
  (ii) 'The longest-running hit of Summer'
'Only in books the flat and final happens'
Lines after Blake: 'Skies by Time are threaded through'

the seventh collection being poems by philip larkin july 1942

'Where should we lie, green heart'
'At the flicker of a letter'
'I am the latest son'
'The wind at creep of dawn'
'This triumph ended in the curtained head'
'The sun swings near the earth'
Leave: 'There was to be dancing'
'As the pool hits the diver, or the white cloud'
'Flesh to flesh was loving from the start'
'If days were matches I would strike the lot'
July miniatures
   'The days, torn single from a sketching-block'
   'If I look till the clouds crack'
   'Summer has broken up'
'Blind through the shouting sun'
The Returning: 'They who are slow to forget death's face'

Sugar and Spice September 1943 [as by 'Brunette Coleman']

The False Friend
Bliss
Femmes Damnées
Ballade des Dames du Temps Jadis
Holidays
The School in August
Fourth Former Loquitur (in MS)

(2) The North Ship (July 1945)

'All catches alight'
'This was your place of birth'
'The moon is full tonight'
Dawn: 'To wake, and hear a cock'
Conscript: 'The ego's country he inherited'
'Kick up the fire'
'The horns of the morning'
Winter: 'In the field, two horses'
'Climbing the hill within the deafening wind'
'Within the dream you said'
Night-Music: 'At one the wind rose'

'Like the train's beat'
'I put my mouth'
Nursery Tale: 'All I remember is'
The Dancer: 'Butterfly'
'The bottle is drunk out by one'
'To write one song, I said'
'If grief could burn out'
Ugly Sister: 'I will climb thirty steps to my room'
'I see a girl dragged by the wrists'
'I dreamed of an out-thrust arm of land'
'One man walking a deserted platform'
'If hands could free you, heart'
'Love, we must part now: do not let it be'
'Morning has spread again'
'This is the first thing'
'Heaviest of flowers, the head'
'Is it for now or for always'
'Pour away that youth'
'So through that unripe day you bore your head'
The North Ship:
    Songs: 65° N 'My sleep is made cold'
        70° N Fortunetelling: 'You will go on a long journey"
        75° N Blizzard: 'Suddenly clouds of snow'
        Above 80° N 'A woman has ten claws'

(3) Unpublished typescript: In the Grip of Light (1947)

'The wind blew all my wedding-day'
'Heaviest of flowers, the head'
Plymouth: 'A box of teak, a box of sandalwood'
'At the chiming of light upon sleep'
'Who whistled for the wind, that it should break'
'Come then to prayers'
'Coming at last to night's most thankful springs'
'Lift through the breaking day'
'Past days of gales'
'I put my mouth'
The quiet one: 'Her hands intend no harm'
Getaway: 'One man walking a deserted platform'
'Many famous feet have trod'
Night-Music: 'At one the wind rose'
To a Very Slow Air: 'The golden sheep are feeding, and'

Träumerei: 'In this dream that dogs me I am part'
'Within the dream, you said'
'Some must employ the scythe'
Winter: 'In the field, two horses'
Deep Analysis: 'I am a woman lying on a leaf'
Thaw: 'Tiny immortal streams are on the move'
Dying day: 'There is an evening coming in'
Two Guitar Pieces: I 'The tin-roofed shack by the railroad'
                  II 'I roll a cigarette, and light'
'And the wave sings because it is moving'

Prefaces to Larkin's Typescript Collections

[from 1st Collection: *Preface]*

It is a debatable point, whether writing about oneself is a more exquisite pleasure than talking about oneself. But the fact that oneself is a subject of the most absorbing interest cannot be disputed by any man, whether he prefer the immediate applause of the conversation, or the more delicate delight of 'long-range confession', as a modern writer puts it.

An illusion that I and my affairs are of some interest, then, is a main motive in this collection of what have become known as the 'Stanley Poems'. But, I flatter myself, it is not the sole one. It is also interesting to note the development in poetic style (and, perhaps, ability) as revealed in the poems, and also – and this, to me, is the most interesting – the attitude towards the subject.

Let us take the poetic style first. It is a source of constant wonder to me that the first poem was written when it was. It is one of the few perfect sonnets I have ever come across. A sense of the most delicate irony pervades all; the 'splintered' thirteenth line is done so well that it is incredible that it was conceived and written offhand in one night. Looking at the original manuscript, I note that lines 1, 7, 8, 9, 12, 15, and 14 went in as they stood without correction.

With the second poem, however, we return to more familiar ground. The emotion is trite, the verse sloppy, with an almost unbearable swing into the good old iambic pentameter for the big finish. The influence of 'Ecclesiastes' is obvious in both matter and style.

I used to think 'The Ships at Mylae' not ineffective. I now think it no better than the others. The effect of 'Ecclesiastes' had worn off, and I returned to the familiar pseudo-Keats babble in which that unforgettably bad poem 'Apollo and Hyacinthus' was written.

'Alvis Victrix' is a vain attempt to regain the touch of the first poem. In almost every department it is inferior.

'Stanley en Musique' was, I suppose, the first authentic Stanley poem. The metre has helped to gain the ironic tone, and its restraint is more than welcome after the preceding outpourings. It also marks my first ventures into the obscure (under the influence of Eliot) and I think it not too incompetent. In the next poem (written almost exactly two months afterwards) consciousness of what I was doing spoilt it, and the lengthening of the last lines of the stanzas induced sentimentality where emotion was desired. 'Erotic Play' is back again in the Eliot metre, more obscure, but as sentimental; while the next poem, in the same metre, is definitely on the way to an ironic pornography.

'Stanley Folâtre' is much more important. Two points distinguish it from the previous poems: the metre, which was entirely original, and the vocabulary and treatment, which was decidedly Auden. The attitude will be mentioned later. Also, I think it to be a model of the elementary 'compressed force' I admire so much. This style steadily increases from this point, but the slobber style had several strong kicks to give yet, including the 'Masque', which is not printed here, and other poems, which are.

'Stanley Gothique' is not important: the technique is, perhaps, unequal to the thought. 'Their seed-time past', on the other hand, is one of the last of the slobber poems. Actually it was the epilogue spoken by the Chorus in the masque, 'Behind the Facade' (a fantastic mixture of slobber and the Auden-Isherwood style).

Passing over the nursery rhyme, the next piece is a curious combination of the slobber and the Auden styles; the stanza is brazenly filched from Auden, but the language is Audenized slobber, and falls vainly.

The remaining poems show a rather easier compromise between the instinctive slobber and the desired 'compressed' styles. The use in these of dissonance is also noticeable, and stanzas are invented with more freedom that [sic] before, although I am never above plagiarising a rhyme-scheme or metre if itsuits the poem I want to write. I regard the presence of 75 single-syllable words in a poem of 84 words ('Take your tomorrow'), however, as being something of a technical achievement.

Turning to the attitude towards the subject, I find myself less at ease. But it may be noted that the emotional attitude does change quite considerably during the space of time in which these poems were written. I will attempt to divide them up.

(1) Plain admiration. (This includes the first four poems.)

(2) Admiration and amusement. The inherent irony of poems I and IV resolved into a cynical amusement of V as the conception of the character 'Stanley' emerged. As
'eyes in which I learn
That I am glad to look, return
My glances every day'*
there was no need at that time to think of themes of death, parting, dust & roses, etc.

(3) Ashes to ashes. This, represented by 'Stanley et la glace', grew into maturity in the immediate post-summer holiday period, when the 'eyes in which I learn that I am glad to look' by no means returned my glances every day. It grew into the Parting theme, strongly stressed by the latter poems of the book, when the war started and I knew that school, even when it did start, would be Stanley-less.

(4) Character. Contemporary with the last two attitudes, a serious conception of the character of 'Stanley' appeared. Stanley was the lord of life, the instinctive barbarian, the magnificent savage. 'Stanley folâtre' [sic] puts this point very clearly, where the connection between the 'frolicking' Stanley and early heroes is indicated. 'Erotic Play', again, gives the conception of Stanley as one who can enjoy his 'scattered time'.

(5) Cooler admiration: the future. The final emotion is a return of the early, unqualified love in a less unbridled form, as well as

---

* [Editor's note] From W. H. Auden's 'Out on the lawn I lie in bed'

a calmer contemplation of the future (although 'Promise' gives a ghastly vision of what may come). The poems are less noisy, more skilfull, yet 'May the passing moon delight . . .' is, in emotion, only a return to 'The Days of thy Youth', with a dash of 'The Ships at Mylae'. The final poem, 'Take Your Tomorrow', is a fusion of love, resignation at parting, the serious Stanley, and the past. Possibly it is the best of them all.

Not all the Stanley poems are included here. Some have been excluded on grounds of inferiority of verse, others, of emotion. Nor are poems addressed to other (and inferior) Stanleys included.

[*from* Poems August 1940: *Foreword*]

This collection of poems was made with no deliberation at all, many poems being printed within a few days of their being written. In consequence, there is much work that is silly, private, careless or just ordinarily bad here. Poems number III, IV, VI, IX, and X are included only to fill up space, not because they are of value.

The keynotes of this collection are Carelessness (=Spontaneity) and Platitudinousness (=Simplicity). The qualities in parentheses are what I aimed at. On the other hand, I like most of the poems here except the ones named above.

August 1940

[*from* Chosen Poems: *Foreword*]

This selection was made from a total mass of about twice as many poems, covering approximately a period of three years (1938–41). They are printed roughly in chronological order, and are generally speaking the original text as it was left at the time.

They are thus selected because as every poet should *like* his poems (not necessarily think them good), I like those I have included enough to want them collected together. Also, I regard the changes that are shown throughout in style as being of interest to the psychologist, if not to the literary critic. They exemplify, to my mind, the natural and to some extent inevitable ossification of a 'boyish gift' with the passing of time, shown by the gradual disappearance of spontaneous verse forms and natural energy, and the accompanying depersonalisation which characterises the later poems. These latter (still speaking from the standpoint of the psychologist) are nearer the poems of a novelist than the poems of a poet.

As for their literary interest, I think that almost any single line by Auden would be worth more than the whole lot put together. The course of ossification, in fact, is concurrent with the gradually increasing traces of the Auden manner (and is possibly the cause of it) until towards the end the poems are to be judged solely by comparison with the Auden of 'Look Stranger!'. Certainly they are not very similar, but Auden's ease and vividness were the qualities I most wished to gain.

The earlier poems, on the other hand, show very little influence at all. Actually I have omitted all extremely early ones,* but they, apart from a little superficial Keats, have no mannerisms. For this reason, perhaps, I think them comparatively successful, and have included five poems from the first selection of poems I ever made.

The significance of the whole collection, however, is uncertain. Obviously the poems are not all of equal merit. Some I included because I liked them wholly; some, because I like one or two lines in them, or because I liked the emotion expressed. Some were written with practically no corrections or consideration, others were carefully premeditated and worked out. But in any case, they will always be of interest to myself, who wrote them, for whom they were written, and for whom this selection is primarily intended.

* [Editor's note] Some of the poems mentioned in this preface are not found in the sole copy of this collection. They are presumably lost.

April, 1941 Warwick

*including a Shakespearean sonnet which began:

'In any garden full of scented blooms
  There will be one rose, most surpassing fair,
O'ertopping every other by its plumes,
  To Summer's crown of glory certain heir . . .'

[*from* SEVEN POEMS]

Another collection, ranging in time from the last one (April 1941) to the end of the year. Surprisingly little produced: I suspect some is lost or not to hand.

Same faults: too much Auden, and all that implies.
P.A.L.

Warwick,
January, 1942.

[*from* The Seventh Collection]

This collection covers the period from April to July the tenth of this year, with the exception of poems II and IV, written in 1940 and 1941 respectively.

Warwick, July 1942.

[*from* Sugar and Spice]
(A Sheaf of Poems by Brunette Coleman:
September 1943)

[The title page has the nursery rhyme: 'What are little boys made of']

These poems were all written in the August and September of this year, and I make no apology for presenting a collection of what may seem 'trivia' in these disturbed times. I feel that now more than ever a firm grasp on the essentials of life is needed.

The two poems with titles in the French language are suggested, of course, by their namesakes by François Villon and Charles Baudelaire, but they are not, of course, 'renderings' in any sense. In my opinion they are improvements.

Finally, I dedicate this slim volume to all my sister-writers, with the exception of Margaret Kennedy, who wrote in *The Constant Nymph*:

'English Schoolgirls are not interesting.'

Brunette Coleman, 1943.

[Note: 'Brunette Coleman' was the name of a fictional female writer, under which name Larkin wrote a number of pieces in prose as well. All the 'Brunette Coleman' work has been collected in *Trouble at Willow Gables and Other Fictions* (London: Faber, 2002), edited by James Booth.]

Note: The Village of the Heart and Further Poems have no prefaces.

APPENDIX 3
SONGS OF INNOCENCE AND
INEXPERIENCE
B. S. Brown.   Edward duCann.   Philip Larkin.
[*The authorship of each item is not indicated*]

MARIE

'Oh Christ!' said God as one day he lay in his armchair of clouds. He was tired of sitting all by himself and it made him feel quite sick to look down into absolute nothingness. So that day he decided to create the universe. That was on the Thursday and afterwards he felt much better. He could now sit and look down at the little worlds. This gave him a great sense of stability. If he did fall there was at least something to fall on to – not of course that he was careless enough to fall.

New things always cease to please after a short while and God was soon feeling pretty sick and empty again. So he did a bit more creating and soon it got quite a hold on him. There seemed no way of losing this rather unpleasant habit of creating.

It was on the Sunday that he created man. He chose that day because naturally he wanted us all to be good Christians. He enjoyed this work of creation more than most as it contained several subtleties. It took a long time to decide what shape to make man. He pondered for a long while on whether man should be square or triangular. Eventually he decided to make him human-shape.

Thus it was that Marie turned out so attractive. She wouldn't have been worth looking at twice if she had been square or triangular. The human, buttock shape was far more subtle and complicated. The men liked her immensely for they loved complication.

Marie had a very pleasant life, she was so nicely shaped. Dozens of men were always pestering her with attention and the shape of her body brought all sorts of peculiar intricacies of relationship. Everyone was in love with her.

This love business rather puzzled God. He had created lust as a purely spiritual thing; he had apportioned out a bit of it to every human being, but love had not entered into his reckonings, and of course he knew nothing about it. Being in the shape of a circle himself love which was essentially a production of the human shaped body did not occur to him.

Still it puzzled and intrigued him until he hit on the cunning idea of having some angels. He decided to step Marie and some of her men friends up to the status of angels. By this time she was rather old, her human body was cracking up. It was too intricate to last long. And God of course did not realise that all love had gone from her and that her husband only affected a show of love.

Marie arrived up in the clouds with amazing rapidity. She seemed to have been hit up there by a fast motor car as she was turning out of a sidestreet on her bicycle. And when she arrived she was quite dizzy being unused to floating in midair. However she soon got used to it; being English she could adapt herself to any unfavourable environment.

At first she was rather lonely and was very relieved when her husband arrived to keep her company. He was a bit shaken too at first, but they soon settled down to the old family routine. However an unfortunate thing happened. As they sat in their cloud armchairs gentle breezes would continually blow Marie's skirts up and over her head. Her husband remembering her early love-tricks thought this was intentional and was deeply shocked. So shocked was he that he severed all contact and went to live on a dirty old rain-cloud.

God had been watching all this and observed that there was no sign of love to be seen. This rather surprised and disappointed him for after all it was to observe love that he had brought them up to heaven.

As a last resort he tried to make love to Marie himself. However she was well past her prime and would not have been attracted very much by a circle even in her younger days. So his attempt fell through.

He was a trifle annoyed and retired to his armchair. However he felt slightly relieved as the only explanation possible was that love had only been a figment of his imagination and not real at all.

So he sat in his cloud and felt happy again.

SOUL

Onward went the ferry,
The oarsman bold in fear's coin:
Nor more was Man mere Man
But twin spirits of dubious worth;
One born still;
The other, whose only birthpangs
Had been the grave of his parent,
Felt Life flow small and novel through his veins;
But set off from the stage,
Unafraid, into death.

BIRTH

Swarming and creeping they made me,
And I stirred in my mother's womb,
Where my body was welded with slowness
And prepared for the death in the tomb.

My body was christened with tear drops
And my slumbers were cradled in sighs;
In sadness my bowels were moulded
With the unseeing knowledge that cries.

Fate rested his hand on my forehead
And his agonies raced in my skull;
With the death beats of time I was branded,
The rollings that nothing can lull.

So when all was finished and fashioned,
And my body had suffered its shape,
While time its last torment was howling
I was born in a land without hope.

THE DEATH OF LIFE

How slowly moves the acrobat
His limbs and lungs are dumb,
For from the circus days of life
The night of death has come.

The giant mountains' shadows move
To join the solemn hearse,
The towers and the trees descend
To see the funeral pass.

And all the woods and animals
Look down at the black ground,
And only raise their fear stained eyes
To see the death that groaned.

And on the bier with blackness
The god of death is crowned,
The symbol of our sadness
To which the world is bound.

– o –

A broken down chair sprawls in the corner;
    Brother I'm coming.
The legs – the one that is left –
Is as useless as a broken matchstick;
    Brother I'm hurrying.
No more romantic symbol
Of happiness alone or in company,
But a hulk of rotting upholstery:
    Brother I'm nearly there.
It no longer has a place
In the glare of the imprisoned fire,
But in a cage with a wilder thing–
A cremation:
    My brother is dead.

To Ursula

What sex-life is there in an English prison?
Such a cacophony of warders, bars and locks
I had never seen;
Though I have felt (and not with a sense of touch)
What convict life must mean;
Disillusion, frustration and abused relief
Without the chance of normal success.
But now – what joy and sanity –
I am in jail in Mexico!

Spoonerism

Ugly, horrid, foul, I am;
I met the virgin at tea;
Angel, sweetness, divinity,
Dare I smile?
I love you, dearest, let me;
My filthy hope is strong,
I'll show you my poems, the little charm
That I unworthy . . .
She spat on the ground where she had stood.

I rode all the way . . .

I rode all the way on the top of a London bus:
When we reached the terminus I rode back again.
I sat in the front like a driver
And turned the people this way and that
In and out of the traffic;
Stopping in time, and ignoring them when the bus was
    full:
Then I went home and played like God with my toys.

INDICES

Index of First Lines

If hands could free you, heart 246
If I look till the clouds crack 183
If I saw the sky in flames 235
Imitating you is fairly easy 127
In a second I knew it was your voice speaking 35
In the field, two horses 239
In the pocket of my blazer 204
In this dream that dogs me I am part 303
'Interesting, but futile,' said his diary 151
Is it for now or for always 248
It is late: the moon regards the city 102
It's no good standing there and looking haughty 203

Kick up the fire, and let the flames break loose 238

Let's go to Stratford-on-Avon, and see a play! 208
Lie there, my tumbled thoughts 45
Lie with me, though the night return outside 282
Lift through the breaking day 284
Like the train's beat 241
Llandovery 189
Lock the door, Lariston, lock it, I say to you 33
Love, we must part now: do not let it be 220

Mantled in grey, the dusk steals slowly in 4
Many famous feet have trod 306
Mary Cox in tennis socks 251
Morning has spread again 221
My sleep is made cold 260
My train draws out, and the last thing I see 230

Nothing significant was really said 62
Now night perfumes lie upon the air 11
Now the shadows that fall from the hills 46
Numberless blades of grass 269

O let the passing moon delight 42
O now, as any other spot in time 186
O today is everywhere 110
O what ails thee, bloody sod 159
Oh see that Fuel Form comin' through the post 188
One man walking a deserted platform 245
Only in books the flat and final happens 158
Out in the lane I pause: the night 137
Out of this came danger 148

Past days of gales 288
Planted deeper than roots 200
Pour away that youth 249
Praise to the higher organisms 48
Prince, fortune is accepted among these rooms 57

Index of Titles